T0305468

From Innovation to Entrepreneurship

From Innovation to Entrepreneurship

Connectivity-based Regional Development

Yasuyuki Motoyama

Ohio State University, USA

Edward Elgar
PUBLISHING

Cheltenham, UK • Northampton, MA, USA

Published by
Edward Elgar Publishing Limited
The Lypiatts
15 Lansdown Road
Cheltenham
Glos GL50 2JA
UK

Edward Elgar Publishing, Inc.
William Pratt House
9 Dewey Court
Northampton
Massachusetts 01060
USA

A catalogue record for this book
is available from the British Library

Library of Congress Control Number: 2019938903

This book is available electronically in the **Elgar**online
Social and Political Science subject collection
DOI 10.4337/9781789901986

ISBN 978 1 78990 197 9 (cased)
ISBN 978 1 78990 198 6 (eBook)

Typeset by Servis Filmsetting Ltd, Stockport, Cheshire

Printed and bound by CPI Group (UK) Ltd, Croydon, CR0 4YY

Contents

List of figures   vi
List of co-authors   vii
Preface   viii
Acknowledgments   xi

1   Introduction: Promoting entrepreneurship, but what kind?   1
2   Why beyond innovation and why entrepreneurship?   8
3   What does the nationwide data say?   27
4   What do entrepreneurs do in the City of Fountains?
    A case study of Kansas City   43
5   How did the Gateway City transform its entrepreneurship?
    A case study of St. Louis   59
6   What information sources do entrepreneurs follow?
    Network analysis with Twitter data   93
7   Conclusion: Beyond innovation to an entrepreneurship
    model   113

Appendix   142
References   146
Index   167

Figures

2.1	Net job creation by firm age in the U.S.	21
3.1	Map of BDS startup rate in all industries	30
3.2	Map of NETS startup rate in high-tech sectors	32
3.3	Map of the *Inc.* high-growth firm ratio	33
3.4	Histogram of three dependent variables	36
3.5	Startup rate in three metro areas and the U.S.	42
5.1	Location of Arch Grants recipients and local support organizations in St. Louis	68
5.2	The network map of Arch Grants recipients and supports	70
6.1	Twitter community map with followers in Kansas City	104
6.2	Twitter network maps with followers in St. Louis	108

Co-authors

Section 4.2: **Heike Mayer**, University of Bern, Switzerland.

Section 4.3: **Arnobio Morelix**, Startup Genome.
Colin Tomkins-Bergh, FoodMaven.

Section 5.2: **Karren Knowlton**, University of Pennsylvania.

Section 5.3: **Jordan Bell-Masterson**, Amazon.
Brian Danley, Swedish University of Agricultural Sciences.
Arnobio Morelix, Startup Genome.
Steven Johnson, St. Louis Regional Economic Development Alliance.
Jim Brasunas, ITEN.
Francis Chmelir, ITEN.

Chapter 6: **Stephan Goetz**, Pennsylvania State University, USA.
Yicheol Han, Pennsylvania State University, USA.

Preface

Like many research projects, this book project started with a personal journey. I have been studying economic development and innovation for the past two decades. During my doctoral program at Berkeley, California, I examined the engineering processes of making innovation at multinational corporations, a study that resulted in my previous book, *Global Companies, Local Innovations* (Motoyama 2012). Despite the current global age, a multinational company must co-locate its research and development (R&D) functions in its core region due to the uncertainty of innovation processes, as well as the engineering and organizational management of those processes.

As a postdoc, I studied the scientific development of nanotechnology and its policy environment. The US federal government enacted the National Nanotechnology Initiative in 2001 to distribute $2 billion per year, justifying the technology initiative for the economic competitiveness of the nation (Motoyama et al. 2011). However, much of the government funding went to basic research at universities. Since it takes years, or even decades, to guide basic research into commercialization, the mechanisms, processes, and effectiveness of the government funding were still in question.

In 2011, my career turned a new corner when I joined the Kauffman Foundation, a philanthropic organization dedicated to the promotion of entrepreneurship. To me, it was a natural extension of my research: I studied innovation at multinational corporations and scientific development at universities. Now is the time to study entrepreneurship which can bridge science, technology, and innovation. I was particularly interested in learning the process of commercializing cutting-edge innovations, like nanotechnology, in the form of entrepreneurship. How do entrepreneurs find such technologies and commercialize them? How do technology transfer offices at universities get involved? How well does the current policy environment support that process?

The Kauffman Foundation opened the door for me to meet a

number of entrepreneurs: from young and bright ones to senior and experienced ones. People who just want to be entrepreneurs and who are struggling to take the first step to start a company. Entrepreneurs who were scaling up companies massively for personal, family, or social reasons. Even accomplished players like Steve Case of AOL, Brad Feld of TechStars, and Jeff Hoffman of Priceline. It is always refreshing to meet and hear from people who are really innovating and driving the economy. In meeting them, I often started with basic and exploratory questions: What is your business? How did you come up with the idea? What kind of challenges did you face and how did you solve them?

It took several months, but I started to find some patterns. And those patterns were unexpected, at least for me at that time. Nobody was using cutting-edge science or engineering technologies, like nanotechnology. Almost nobody mentioned patents. No company came out of universities. Well, not exactly – some entrepreneurs did use cutting-edge technology and had patents that came out of universities, but they were only a few out of a couple of hundred. Clearly, those were rather exceptions than the norm, and something else was going on. My research questions about technology and commercialization were not answered, or rather my questions were missing and did not fit the big picture in entrepreneurship. Entrepreneurs were not the people to discover or dig out cutting-edge technologies to commercialize them, but they were the ones to envision markets by identifying something that did not exist before or where nobody was offering anything better. Of course, entrepreneurs used various technologies, but not necessarily cutting-edge ones. There were many ways to run businesses, and entrepreneurs were the people who could find available technologies and combine them to make things happen. In other words, more than 90 percent of cases I have observed told me that technology did not create markets or businesses. Entrepreneurs created markets. Then, entrepreneurs later found technologies to make their businesses and markets happen.

As mentioned, this finding was unexpected, because that is not what the currently dominant theory of innovation suggests, or how the policy is framed. Under the current theory, innovation will occur after scientific development takes place. The process is, or should be, straightforward and linear: The government funds a university for scientific research. Researchers develop cutting-edge technologies. Universities make those technologies available, but protect the intellectual property with patents. Technology transfer offices at universities mediate among entrepreneurs, companies, and industries that ultimately use those technologies for their own products and services.

In short, the model that current innovation theory and policy promotes does not fit most of entrepreneurship, but targets a small minority of business development. To be fair, there are cases that the current innovation theory fits. For instance, in the pharmaceutical industry, a company can import a newly formulated drug from a university and mass-produce it for consumers. That company requires an initial investment of millions to conduct lab experiments and survive the lengthy review by the Food and Drug Administration (FDA). Alternatively, you hear stories about how the Defense Advanced Research Project Agency (DARPA) created the Internet (Zook 2005; Greenstein 2015) or how Google, Yahoo, and Cisco came out of universities. However, these stories are uncritically retold (Lester 2005) without examining whether or what kind of technologies these companies used from Stanford University, or how commonly such cases occur.

Motivated to investigate this theme deeply, I organized several research projects to examine the questions quantitatively with nation-wide data and explore qualitatively with multiple regional cases. I was fortunate to have several collaborators on different projects and to have excellent research assistants at Kauffman. This book synthesizes our findings and presents an alternative model of economic development based on entrepreneurship.

Acknowledgments

This book would not have been possible without help from so many friends and colleagues. It may be unconventional to thank co-authors, but I would like to because their ideas made this book better: Heike Mayer, Arnobio Morelix, Colin Tomkins-Bergh, Karren Knowlton, Jim Brasunas, Steve Johnson, Stephan Goetz, and Yichael Han.

I had rare opportunities to present my book project at several Japanese universities even from an early stage, and their feedback was essential to improve my manuscript: For this I thank Manao Kidachi and Kappei Hidaka at Chuo University; Tetsutaro Okada at Kagawa University; Takeshi Fujimoto, Masanori Namba, and Kanichiro Suzuki at Ritsumeikan Asia Pacific University. In addition, Ben Spigel and Fumi Kitagawa at the University of Edinburgh, as well as Thomas Funke at RKW in Frankfurt, gave me opportunities to present at their universities. Emil Malizia kindly hosted a seminar at the University of North Carolina, and I appreciate feedback from Maryann Feldman, Nichola Lowe, Bill Lester, Mary Donegan, and others. In addition, Emil Malizia has been a great collaborator, scholar, and mentor throughout past research projects. Thanks to Richard Freeman for letting me present at Harvard Business School.

I would also like to thank my former Kauffman colleagues. Dane Stangler was a visionary leader who supported my research from the very beginning. Jason Wiens and Evan Absher taught me how policymakers think and how we can talk to them. Rachel Carlton and Jonathan Robinson kept me engaged with entrepreneurship practitioners. Kate Maxwell, Jared Konzcal, Arnobio Morelix, Jordan Bell-Masterson, Alex Krause, Chris Jackson, and Emily Fetsch were bright research assistants. It was always fun to bounce book ideas to each other with Sam Arbesman. Michelle St. Clair and Mette Cramer took care of me in every unfilled dimension. Suren Dutia opened doors for me in St. Louis.

I am grateful to my former colleagues at the University of Kansas for their intellectual and spiritual support: Nate Brunsell,

Jay Johnson, Shannon O'Lear, Barney Warf, and Alex Diener. Sarah Gowen and Beth Chapple patiently reviewed my manuscript. Katy Crossan was the most efficient acquisition editor. I am also grateful for my new colleagues at Ohio State University, and their inputs in February 2018 were helpful to finalize my manuscript. Ed Malecki and Ned Hill were great mentors.

Last but not least, I would like to thank my family for their love and patience. My parents did not mind listening to their son's geeky talk even when he was unstoppable. Kai and Elyse gave me smiles and a meaning of life every day. My wife, Michelle, was always the first and last person that I could talk about any research idea, good or bad, and, she guided me in the right way in my life.

November 2018
Columbus, Ohio

1. Introduction: Promoting entrepreneurship, but what kind?

1.1 A TALE OF TWO ENTREPRENEURS

Joe Anderson has finally taken his first step as an entrepreneur. He opened his first office at the Cambridge Innovation Center (CIC) in St. Louis, Missouri. The facility is a glass-walled building funded by a local private university and the City of St. Louis. His 2,000-square-foot office space is not large but spacious enough for now, and he will use one half of the open space as lab space and the other half as workstation space. He envisions being able to seat three to four people easily and having a meeting space with a whiteboard, glass wall, and projector.

Joe's niche in business is cutting-edge nanotechnology. With his background in chemistry, he has been a postdoctoral researcher at a local private university for the past four years and worked on various nanotechnology projects for a physics professor. The professor invented the Plasma Shower Method to include a lithium atom inside a molecule made only of carbons. This carbon-made "buckyball," or C_{60} fullerene to use the technical term, is the hardest material on earth, like carbon nanotubes or diamonds, and will hold its shape and characteristics under any external shocks except fires. Including a lithium atom inside was novel because the lithium holding C_{60} will be negatively charged and can form a very stable molecule with a positively charged atom. It will be a source for new materials that can be used for, literally, anything.

During his postdoctoral tenure, Joe and his professor filed several patents, and the US Patent and Trademark Office (USPTO) officially granted the first patent two months ago. Then, last month, Joe applied for a small startup fund from his university, which was initiated by the university's provost office several years ago to increase its commitment to the local economy. The $100,000 award is only the beginning, and Joe has a financing plan. He will apply for Small Business Innovation Research (SBIR) grants from the federal government in a year or two and seek venture capital funds in three to four years. Now, he needs to concentrate on successfully mass-producing the carbon-made molecule. His background is ideal because he can extract the right molecule using his chemical method, with which he has had initial success in the past year. In about two years, Joe anticipates he will start selling his molecule products to major chemical, petroleum, and likely pharmaceutical companies.

Charlie Hopp is also about to start his business, but in a very different style. Ever since he attended the Startup Weekend in St. Louis two years ago, an event at which attendees form a business plan within 54 hours, Charlie has been fascinated by the idea of starting his own business. He did not have a business idea then, so he has just joined another group for the weekend. He has been looking for his idea for two years and thinks he has finally found one: A background check service for employers.

Charlie studied political science as an undergraduate with the intention of advancing to law school, but he decided that was not his path. However, he became involved with a research project about criminal background checks and found it was a nightmare to identify comprehensive background records because the court and legal systems' technologies in this area were extremely backward. In theory, most such information is publicly accessible, but courts maintain and present each type of information – that is, violence, felony, traffic violations, and so on – in a different way, often through paper documents. There was no online system to obtain all this information, with the exception of the sex offender registry. He has repeatedly heard from friends working in human resources about this need for more comprehensive background information to be available. An employer might investigate the record of one or two individuals or hire a detective, but not when hiring dozens or hundreds of new employees: It would be an extremely labor-intensive process of navigating through different documents, city, county, and state-level courts, and integrating information from different police and court branches.

Charlie currently works for Express Scripts, a major pharmacy benefits management company in St. Louis, and has gained a little familiarity with the company's large database. But he knows that he is not a trained software engineer, so he has been partnering with an engineer who was also part of Startup Weekend two years ago. In the next three months, the two will keep their day jobs and work nights and weekends to develop the business. Their goal is to come up with the first version of the background system within three months, and Charlie plans to begin service to a few local companies where his friends have informed him of the need. Charlie and his partner have no plan to seek or receive external funds. They will develop the database first and consider hiring people after they make the first sales – a classic case of bootstrapping.

For this entrepreneurial activity, Charlie and his partner work between home and their new "office," which is not a traditional company office, but a cubical space Charlie is renting at T-REX, a so-called co-working space in downtown St. Louis. T-REX occupies five floors in a commercial building with 160,000 square feet, and provides "low-cost and flexible enterprise space" (T-REX 2017). This open-space facility is home to 110 startup companies and several entrepreneurship support organizations. The rent for a workstation space is $75 monthly, but what Charlie values most are the events organized by T-REX, such as a guest speaker series, and the constant interaction with other entrepreneurial-minded people.

This is a tale of two entrepreneurs working very different styles. Two important questions to ask: Which entrepreneur is likely to succeed? Which entrepreneur should the public sector support? One is a scientist with knowledge of cutting-edge nanotechnology; the other is an ordinary college graduate. One is setting up his base with support from his professor at a state-of-the-art incubator, while the other is more or less informally starting the entrepreneurial journey with his engineer partner at a co-working space and at home. One already has funding and a patent, while the other has no funding and no plans to pursue a patent. In short, Joe Anderson is a classic example of the 21st-century entrepreneur most innovation theories would support. Charlie Hopp, in contrast, is a casual entrepreneur who may fail or succeed, and his life will still go on. The answer, then, seems obvious: If you were an investor, you would bet on Joe Anderson, or his kind of entrepreneurship, as most likely to succeed. Who cares about Charlie Hopp?

We should start here with the crude baseline fact that neither of these two companies may exist five years from now. There is a 5-50 rule in entrepreneurship: just about 50 percent of companies survive five years. This pattern has been consistent across different industries and locations for the last 25 years, even during the Great Recession years since 2008 (SBA 2011; Bureau of Labor Statistics 2017). Yes, starting and running a successful new company is just like tossing a coin.

Setting this fact aside, we start this book with our bold hypothesis that the real answer to "Which entrepreneur?" is Charlie, the casual entrepreneur. The answer to the question why is the main theme we will explore in this book. Unmasking these reasons has many important implications in practice: What kind of support environment do entrepreneurs need? How might the public and non-profit sectors support entrepreneurship? Moreover, it has critical implications for the theories of innovations and entrepreneurship.

1.2   PLAN OF THE BOOK

The fundamental premise of this book is that entrepreneurship is about people – entrepreneurs. You will see how individual entrepreneurs learn the process of starting, running, and growing businesses. Contrary to the dominant theories of innovation, we do not find that scientific knowledge or cutting-edge technologies spill over to entrepreneurial activities, at least not easily, even if entrepreneurs, universities, and venture funds co-exist in the same region. Instead, the spillover of knowledge takes place between people, primarily entrepreneurs, and there must be specific social and organizational mechanisms to make it happen.

This finding draws from another premise. In entrepreneurship and innovation, there is no single right answer. Since entrepreneurs are the people to offer commercial value by trying something new, there are a million different ways to make it happen. Also, whatever the brilliant idea is, the original business plan by an entrepreneur may not (and usually does not) work right. The entrepreneur has to experiment and adjust continually. In this circumstance, you cannot pick winners or structure the most efficient plan in a linear way. Instead, continuous learning, primarily from other local entrepreneurs and active supporters, is the crucial information source for entrepreneurs. In this localized feedback mechanism, entrepreneurs obtain an array of knowledge about how to start and develop their businesses. For instance, how to define the market, how to define your product, and how to sell your product are all different skills. Entrepreneurs also need to learn how to manage their company's finance (not necessarily finding venture capitals or investors), how to hire people, how to fire people, how to communicate with employees, how to incentivize employees, and so on. In addition, they need to learn how to balance their work life and private life. In other words, it is everything about how to run your business, and there are no born-to-be entrepreneurs. They have to keep learning as their businesses grow and their markets change.

In this book, we triangulate various data to investigate entrepreneurship at the individual and regional levels. While it is not easy to measure innovations and entrepreneurship, we employ different quantitative data to get as close as possible to the core of these two topics. We further supplement with rich qualitative data.

Chapter 2 reviews theories of innovation and entrepreneurship, which are considered the two most critical sources of economic development and which most scholars treat as two sides of the same coin. However, as we disentangle these concepts, we demonstrate that innovation studies are biased toward high-tech sectors and primarily examine inputs of innovation, such as R&D activities, science and engineering workforce, and patents, and are weak to connect the mechanism that links inputs to outputs. Instead, we propose to examine entrepreneurship as the driver of economic development by assuming that entrepreneurship requires a different set of inputs and resources from innovation.

In Chapter 3, we examine the quantitative dimension of entrepreneurship at the metropolitan level throughout the U.S. We discuss various measures of entrepreneurship. As with innovations, there is no perfect measure for entrepreneurship. Each measure comes with major pros and cons. To overcome those limitations, we employ three kinds of entrepreneurship measures as dependent variables and analyze regional factors. We demonstrate that research activities, patents, and funding, the core components in the innovation theories, have no statistical relationship to entrepreneurship rates. Instead, we find that education-related human capital factors are important.

Chapters 4 and 5 further explore those human capital factors in the context of entrepreneurship through in-depth regional studies in Kansas City and St. Louis. The cases of these two cities allow us to examine the local system of entrepreneurship beyond Silicon Valley and Boston, the regions that are both most frequently studied and dominated by world-class universities and the previous innovation studies. Theorizing based on anomalies is not the most effective way to understand how entrepreneurship works in hundreds of more typical regions. Kansas City and St. Louis each have a relatively high level of entrepreneurship, according to the Business Dynamics Statistics (Census Bureau 2016), and they have experienced remarkable transformations in entrepreneurship activities over the past few years.

Chapter 4 features the case of Kansas City, the City of the Fountains famous for barbecue. Little known outside, this city has planned entrepreneurship as one of the economic pillars of the region. In 2012, the regional chamber of commerce launched the Big Five Initiative, with one of its goals being to promote entrepreneurship (Greater Kansas City Chamber 2011). Kansas City is the home of the Kauffman Foundation, a $2 billion philanthropic organization dedicated to the promotion of entrepreneurship, and the legacy of its founder, Ewing Marion Kauffman, is still present today through spin-offs from his pharmaceutical company, the Marion Labs, and through mentorship. We use a survey of more than 200 companies in the so-called high-tech sectors, and identify that Kansas City companies value access to high-quality people and mentors as the sources of company growth instead of access to research and universities. Then, based on interviews and focus groups, we analyze how and why people participate in 1 Million Cups, a weekly interactive session between entrepreneurs and audience, which starts to demonstrate more learning process by entrepreneurs.

Chapter 5 presents the somewhat different approach to entrepreneurship espoused by St. Louis. St. Louis has enjoyed the legacy of the transportation and manufacturing sectors, but those industries have suffered numerous closures and relocations in the past 20 years and never regained their strength. As a result, political and civic leaders had come to realize by 2010 that reliance on old and "anchor" companies was not their answer, but that entrepreneurship and immigrants were. They have since created a regionwide business plan competition that not only distributed a pool of money to growth-oriented companies, but also cultivated an infrastructure and networks for entrepreneurs and supporting organizations. We explore how these startup entrepreneurs are growing, staying connected, and continuing their learning. In addition, we interview high-growth Inc. companies which have achieved millions in revenue and demonstrate how such learning continues throughout different stages of business development.

In Chapter 6, we expand our scope to a substantially larger regional scale by analyzing open-access Twitter accounts. We identify 255 Twitter accounts of entrepreneurship-related support organizations in Kansas City and St. Louis, as well as 130 accounts nationally, allowing us to trace network patterns of more than 250,000 followers. We analyze what popular Twitter accounts those entrepreneurs follow, which accounts overlap within each region, and between the region and nation.

Chapter 7 synthesizes Chapters 3 through 6 and derives theory and policy implications from the findings. While the entrepreneurship model requires constant adjustment and learning, the currently dominant approach to promoting innovation is based on the so-called linear model of development (Godin 2006). This linear model assumes that scientific discovery (basic research) is essential to society and that ideas will go through applied research and become commercialized. The role of government in this model is to fill the "valley of death" by funding scientific research at universities and making initial venture funds available when venture capital firms and the private sector are not yet willing to provide funds (Auerswald and Branscomb 2003). This approach of picking winners through the public or semi-public sectors is incompatible with and ineffective for the "experiment and adjust" model of entrepreneurship that is uncovered throughout this book. This final chapter further discusses this alternative entrepreneurship model and potential approaches available to the public and non-public sectors to promote entrepreneurship.

2. Why beyond innovation and why entrepreneurship?

2.1 CONCEPT OF INNOVATIONS AND ENTREPRENEURSHIP

As in any academic discipline, scholars who study economics hardly agree on what is important. John Quigley, an economist at the University of California, Berkeley, once said that if you gather thousands of economists at American Economic Association annual meetings, there are only two things on which they can agree: Rent control is bad; trade is good (Quigley 2002). We may add two more things: Innovations and entrepreneurship are important for the development of the economy.

However, we face an immediate challenge when we begin to refine what we mean by, and how we measure, innovations and entrepreneurship. The mainstream neoclassical economics unfortunately provide only a generic definition of the first term, innovations (Isard 1956; Lundvall and Maskell 2000): Shifting economic resources out of an area of lower and into an area of higher productivity and greater yield (Buss 2001, 188; *Economist* 2009). It is a fine observation at the macroeconomic level, but does not provide the explanatory power to answer the question: How can we make innovations, or "higher productivity" activities?

Throughout this book, we use the scope of innovations pioneered by Schumpeter and his followers. Thus, innovations are new (or a combination of new and old) activities and can take many forms, such as new products, new methods of production, new systems, or new markets (Schumpeter 1934 [2012], 66). They can be technological or organizational (Edquist et al. 2001).

One critical dimension of innovations is that it is not a synonym of invention, a creation of something that did not exist before. Here, Schumpeter provided an insightful observation in the early twentieth century:

[Innovation] in particular must hence be distinguished from "invention." As long as they are not carried into practice, inventions are economically irrelevant. And to carry any improvement into effect is a task entirely different from the invention of it, and a task, moreover, requiring entirely different kinds of aptitudes. . . It is, therefore, not advisable, and it may be downright misleading, to stress the element of invention as much as many writers do. (Schumpeter 1934 [2012], 88–9)

In sum, innovations are new things and have commercial values (Freeman 1982; Edquist 2005). We explore how these two conditions will reshape the debate about innovations in the rest of the book.

The second term, entrepreneurship, faces an equal or even greater challenge of definition. Schumpeter described it as "the carrying out of new combinations that constitutes the entrepreneur, it is not necessary that he should be permanently connected with an individual firm; many 'financiers,' 'promoters,' and so forth are not" (1934 [2012], 75). Thus, similar to his concept of innovations, Schumpeter differentiated inventors or capitalists from entrepreneurs (1934 [2012], 89).

At the same time, this definition of entrepreneur by Schumpeter as someone who carries out innovations not only provided an advantage to wide interpretation, but also created a gray area between innovations and entrepreneurship. In other words, what he defined as an entrepreneur was rather an "innovator" who might create his own company to sell his innovations or generate new products from within an existing large company (Allen 1991; Sledzik 2013). Mark Frank, an economic historian, argued that such dichotomous dimensions reflected the two periods and two thoughts of Schumpeter: His earlier work focused on small firms as isolated, romanticized individual actors who challenged the social system, based on his European experiences. His later work, then, concerned large established corporations with monopolistic competition and agglomerations capable of fulfilling the entrepreneurial function, reflecting his time in America (Frank 1998, 505).

This mixture of innovation and entrepreneurship has created a legacy, and some confusion, among academic works discussing innovation and entrepreneurship under economic development. We can see such confusion even in the writing of an influential thinker like Peter Drucker:

"Innovation" and "entrepreneurship" have become "buzz words" in the ten years since this book was written and first published. . . It requires that the business itself be organized to be a successful innovator. It requires both a discipline of innovation and a discipline of entrepreneurship that is a discipline how to make innovation effective in the market place. *And this is what this book is all about.* (1985 [2015], i, emphasis in original)

Drucker was correct to point out that innovation and entrepreneurship have become buzzwords, and he himself has difficulty in differentiating between innovation and entrepreneurship or between innovator and entrepreneur. In short, even within the academic literature about innovations and entrepreneurship, these two concepts have become practically synonymous. An entrepreneur is de facto an innovator, that is, one who creates innovations under all circumstances, whether at a new firm or a large established firm. In the next section, we will observe how this overlap between innovation and entrepreneurship shaped the development of innovation theories.

2.2   SYSTEMS OF INNOVATION THEORY

How can we generate more innovations? For this simple, important question, neoclassical economics, the mainstream discipline of economics, again provides no practical answer as described earlier. The neoclassical economists perceive that the economy is run by atoms of individuals and firms motivated by profit maximization. Some innovations, or technological change, are brought in by external shocks, in their view. In other words, major innovations, which cannot be modeled mathematically, happen through accidents and do not fit into the neoclassicals' primary interest in identifying the optimal points.

In contrast, innovation theorists start with an observation that modern economic growth came in waves, such as following the advent of the steam engine in the 1770s, railways in the 1820s, and automobiles and mass production in the 1900s (Kondratiev 1924; Schumpeter 1939, 1954). These waves of economic growth were concentrated not only in terms of rapid and continuous time frames, but also in terms of locations of emerging innovations. This observation led to the premise of innovation theorists that individuals or firms do not innovate in isolation but in collaboration with other organizations, and such interdependence with other organizations forms a broader system to generate innovations. For Nelson (1993), Etzkowitz and

Leydesdorff (2000), and Etzkowitz (2008), those interdependent innovation actors were organizations supporting R&D, such as large corporations, universities, and government labs. More broadly, Lundvall (1992) perceived the interdependence broadly through other firms (suppliers, customers, competitors, and so on) or non-firm entities such as universities, schools, and government ministries (Freeman 2002). Edquist (1997, 2005) and Lundvall (2010) further argued that the behavior of innovation actors, and hence the rate and direction of innovations, were also shaped by institutions such as laws, rules, norms, and routines that constitute incentives or obstacles for innovation. In sum, these systems of innovation theorists perceived that there were some sets of systems and sets of innovation actors that were better suited to produce more innovations.

While the scope of this system of innovation study was at the national scale, a group of scholars started to develop an equivalent framework at the regional scale at around the same time (the Regional Innovation System). Based on their observation that innovative firms of the same industry tended to be geographically clustered (Porter 1990), they considered the region to be the level at which the production and innovation system was organized (Cooke 1992, 1998, 2001; Asheim 1996; Asheim and Isaksen 1997). This regional focus allowed them to empirically analyze the system of industry production and innovation closely, and they investigated how different regions organized production inputs (such as qualified labor force, direct investment, funding) affected some forms of economic outputs related to innovations (such as GDP per capita, Gross Expenditure on R&D (GERD), the formation of important industries (often high-tech sectors), and the level of technology transfer (Cooke 1998).

Whether nationally or regionally focused, these system of innovation theories placed innovations and knowledge creation at the center. This focus further allowed innovations to be perceived not as an exogenous factor to the economy, but as an endogenous factor that a given economic system could produce and redevelop. In the analytical process, the systems approach employed historical and evolutionary perspectives and detached from the optimality calculation emphasized by the neoclassicals. In other words, the systems approach underscored the importance of interdependence and the role of institutions, and argued for the nonlinearity of innovation systems. It allowed us to understand different forms of production and innovation systems.

At the same time, the systems approach has been criticized as functioning not as a formal theory, as it did not provide specific propositions to explain which systems could produce more innovations, but rather as a framework to understand different innovation systems (Liu and White 2001; Edquist 2005). Similarly, the Regional Innovation System approach did not have the power to explain what kind of regions could produce more innovations. Moreover, its focus was on technology transfer activities, not how innovations were created or how different firms or industrial clusters identified new commercial opportunities.

2.3 KNOWLEDGE SPILLOVER LITERATURE

In the 1990s when the systems of innovation approach was becoming influential, another discipline set emerged to investigate the question of which region could generate more innovations by centrally examining the role of knowledge spillovers in the creation of innovations. These knowledge spillover studies started with the seminal works by Jaffe and colleagues (1993), and Jaffe and Trajtenberg (1996, 2002) which analyzed the patent citation patterns and uncovered that inventors with a higher productivity of patent production were more likely to cite each other if they were located in the same geographic area, such as the same metropolitan area. This citation pattern was observed with patents in electronics, optics, and nuclear technologies. Based on the same methodology, Almeida and Kogut (1997) observed the same pattern in the semiconductor industry. Zucker, Darby, and their colleagues (1996, 1998, 2007) employed a different method, identifying "star scientists" in the bioscience fields and their engagement with industry research, yet came to the same conclusion.

In contrast to the systems of innovation works, the knowledge spillover studies advanced understanding of innovation outputs and regional characteristics, providing the predictive power regarding which regions had the potential to produce more innovations. In short, the studies found that innovations were linked to research and development activities at the university and industry levels, a pool of highly skilled labor, and the concentration, and hence competition, of firms in the same high-tech sector (Acs et al. 1994b; Anselin et al. 1997; Feldman 2000). The production level of patents was the usual output. Feldman and Florida (1994) and Audretsch and Feldman

(1996) further used the product development data from the US Small Business Administration (SBA), and reached essentially the same conclusion. We review these measures of innovation and their limitations later in this chapter.

More recent studies of innovation uncovered so-called "open innovation" systems in which formal institutions, such as governments, universities, and industry, play lesser roles, but vertical collaboration between technology developers, customers, and end users induced technological improvements (Chesbrough et al. 2006; Gassman 2006; Parida et al. 2012). Examples of these technological innovations include the Linux operating system (Weber 2004), computer games (Prügl and Schreier 2006), mobile service (Mahr and Lievens 2012), and medical equipment (Lettl, Herstatt, and Gemuenden 2006).

While these open innovation studies emphasized the importance of end user innovation (Franke et al. 2016), which was also observed in development of scientific instrument (Von Hippel 1976, Von Hippel and Katz 2002; Mody 2006), at this moment, however, they provide little connection to entrepreneurship, which starts with a specific process to identify commercialization opportunities. In other words, open innovation can improve technologies, but does not necessarily lead to a formation of a company or companies. As discussed earlier, entrepreneurs are a special kind of people who make this commercialization happen by developing and using new technologies, as well as forming a company and operating an organization between these processes. This strategic process is critical because technologies themselves do not induce economic development or wealth, but must be embedded in economic and industrial forms. Corporations are the fundamental unit of these economic forms under modern capitalism, and, through corporations with strategic objectives, entrepreneurs exercise their operations, generate wealth, and reinvest in further economic activities. This is a long and challenging process that we cannot ignore. In short, we need further understanding about how entrepreneurship, either through individuals or corporations, takes place. If particular locals promote entrepreneurship better than others, it is critical to understand how that local system for entrepreneurship functions.

2.4 MEASURING INNOVATIONS AND ITS LIMITATIONS

As reviewed, there has been some advancement in understanding innovations and their creation. The systems of innovation theory expanded the knowledge of what kinds of actors and institutions are involved in the broader innovation-making activities, whereas the knowledge spillover theory assessed what kind of place-based factors are associated with higher innovation activities. However, scholars have always faced a challenge here. It is extremely difficult to quantify and measure innovations: "[A] fundamental definitional issue is what we actually mean by 'new'. Does an innovation have to contain a basic new principle that has never been used in the world before, or does it only need to be new to a firm? Does an innovation have to incorporate a radically novel idea, or only an incremental change?" (Smith 2005, 149).

Given this issue, it is important to review types of innovation measures on which scholars have relied in the past. The first type, oriented to capture R&D activities, originated from the Frascati Manual of the Organisation for Economic Co-operation and Development[1] (OECD) in 1963 and has been continually updated to the current seventh edition in 2002. This approach considers that innovations come from the production of "new" knowledge and "new" practical applications of knowledge in the forms of basic research, applied research, and experimental development. Statistically, they measure 1) the personnel involved in R&D (or person-years spent on R&D), 2) expenditure on R&D, such as labor and capital costs, 3) resources transferred, and 4) acquisition and other grant costs (OECD 2002).

Since this approach "is devoted to measuring R&D inputs" (OECD 2002, 17), its limitation lies in its neglect of innovation outputs (Kleinknecht and Mohnen 2002). It assumes that the more

---

[1] It is important to footnote that the efforts to collect data by the National Science Foundation (NSF) in the 1950s predated the OECD approach. With its mandate to measure scientific and technological activities in the U.S. (Godin 2003), NSF produced "systematic" and "comprehensive" annual reports to cover all research and development activities by the federal government, industry, nonprofit institutions, and other manpower; exchange; and the state of scientific information (NSF 1953). In addition to the R&D expenditure, the NSF collected what they considered "outputs" of scientific and technological activities, such as publications, patents, and spin-offs (NSF 2012). We review consequences of these data-tracking efforts in Chapter 7.

R&D inputs there are, whether in forms of expenditure or personnel, the more innovations will come out, clearly neglecting the dimension of efficiency. This measure may apply better when a company, industry, or a country is catching up by imitating the market leader, such as Japan in the 1980s and South Korea in the 1990s. However, imitation or assembling large-scale inputs does not guarantee that it will produce innovations. It does not lead to profits or market survival, either, when competitors mobilize the high level of R&D inputs but compete for the same product, such as the case of dynamic random-access memory (DRAM) by US and Japanese semiconductor firms in the 1980s and 1990s.

The second type is a derivative of the first one, but applies to the intensity of R&D at the industry level. This approach analyzes the proportion of revenue that goes toward R&D expenditure and calculates the industrial average. Then, it classifies industries into the three levels of R&D intensity: the high-intensity (or high-tech) industries spend more than 5 percent of revenue toward R&D activities, the medium-intensity industries spend between 1 and 5 percent, and the low-intensity industries spend less than 1 percent (OECD 1997). Often, the high-tech industries are information technology (including semiconductor and computer equipment, telecommunications, and software), pharmaceutical and biotechnology, aerospace, and precision machinery (DeVol et al. 2009). The medium-tech industries are the motor vehicle and various chemical, petroleum, and mineral product sectors. The low-tech industries are in the paper, food, and wood and textile sectors (OECD 1997). In short, this approach assumes that the industries with higher R&D intensity produce more innovations and analyzes how the high-tech sector is structured or grows.

The limitation of this approach is similar to that of the first approach: it assumes that the higher intensity of R&D inputs will yield more innovations, and it also assumes that the level of innovation can be observed uniformly at the industry level. Such assumptions cannot reconcile with the fact that some companies in the high-tech sectors will inevitably become bankrupt. Moreover, the growth of employment or productivity in high-tech sectors has been slower than the overall economy since the 1990s (Kask and Sieber 2002; Hecker 2005). This creates an empirical paradox that high-tech industries can be innovation-oriented yet experience slower growth. As Michael Porter famously put it, "In fact, there is no such thing as a low-tech industry. There are only low-tech companies—that

is, companies that fail to use world-class technology and practices to enhance productivity and innovation" (Porter 1998, 86).
Alternatively many companies in what are classified as "low-tech"
industries can continue to innovate, generate wealth for a long and
sustained period, such as Coca-Cola, Procter & Gamble, Hallmark,
Kroger, and so on (Collins 2001). We simply cannot ignore innovative
products or companies outside of the "high-tech" sectors.

The third type of innovation measure traces patents, a public
contract between an inventor and the government to "exclude
others from making, using, offering for sale, or selling the invention" (USPTO 2015). In theory, this patent system should provide
an incentive to the inventor because he or she can monopolize the
use and profits from it. The patent application and grant data are
publicly available and list all inventors (who create the technical
novelty), applicants (who submit the application), and classification
of technologies, detailed locations, and citations. The numbers of
applied and granted patents were particularly large – 589,410 and
298,407 respectively – for utility patents in 2015 (USPTO 2016),
which allows sophisticated geographic and network analysis on a
longitudinal basis.

While the innovation studies using patent data have increased
exponentially in the last 20 years, the limitations of this data may
be underemphasized. Some pioneering scholars in this methodology
have cautioned the use of patents as a "valid but noisy measure"
(Jaffe et al. 1998, 183), and it is worth highlighting those limitations.
First, only a fraction of innovations are patented, and, moreover,
there are many variations within this fraction of industry, firm, and
time (Griliches et al. 1991). That is, some industries and companies
may be innovative, but do not file patents at all. In other cases, firms
will not commercialize their patent, but use it to prevent business
and research activities of other companies related to the technology
(Kleinknecht and Mohnen 2002). In other words, even if filed and
granted, patents do not signify the innovativeness. Second, patents
are an indicator of invention rather than innovation, that is, a new
technical principle and not a commercial innovation (Freeman 1982;
Feldman 2000). Therefore, a company, a region, or an industry
with many patents may have little commercial value. IBM is the
best example here. It has consistently been the number one patent
producer in the world for the past two decades (see Table 2.2 later in
the chapter), but it has faced major financial difficulties.

Third, even if we accept that patents are a reasonable measure of innovation outputs, the commercial value of patents is extremely skewed (Griliches 1992); only a small fraction of patents produce a large volume of profits, and the majority have little or no value (Bessen and Meurer 2008). There has not been a systematic review of patent values, and estimates range from 75 percent (Griliches 1990) to 90 percent (Mowery 2009) of US patents having no commercial value. Similarly, Carlsson and Fridh (2002) and Braunerhjelm et al. (2010) reported that only 1 to 2 percent of patents produce notable commercial value. Thus, patents could be a meaningful measure if we could identify only the ones with high commercial value, as the sheer number or citation of patents do not reflect innovations, let alone applied patents versus granted patents.

The fourth type of innovation measure is based on surveys and focuses on new products at the firm level. The Science Policy Research Unit (SPRU) at the University of Sussex mobilized a panel of about 400 technical experts to identify major innovations across all sectors and identified about 4,300 innovations in Europe from 1945 to 1983 (Smith 2005). The US SBA developed a similar database through an examination of about 100 engineering and trade journals and identified 4,200 innovations made by small businesses in 1982 (Acs and Audretsch 1990; Audretsch and Feldman 1996).

The limitation of this approach is its focus on product innovations, which are relatively easy to identify but represent only one segment of innovations. Other types of innovations, such as process or system innovations, are excluded. For instance, Toyota is known for its efficient production system (Liker 2004), but that strength would not be included in this approach, which instead would count only the types of new cars. In addition, these databases include limited years only and are by now outdated.[2]

2.5   SUMMARY OF INNOVATION MEASURES AND LIMITATIONS

Given the inherent difficulty of measuring innovations, scholars have employed various indicators related to mostly innovation input

---

[2]   Although there are efforts at the US SBA to develop another round of this kind of database.

Table 2.1   Summary of innovation measures

Measure	Type	Limitations
R&D expenditure & personnel	Inputs	Assumes more research produces innovations
High-tech industry	Inputs	Assumes industry-wide research intensity reflects innovations
Patents	Quasi-outputs	Excludes non-patented innovations; Most have no commercial value
Surveys	Outputs	Focuses only on new products; Outdated

Source: Author's review; Acs et al. 2002; Ratanawaraha and Polenske 2007.

activities (and some limited outputs), and each method has major limitations. As summarized in Table 2.1, innovation input measures, such as R&D expenditure or industry R&D intensity, do not measure outputs; patents are only a rough measure of outputs and exclude many innovations that are not patented; and surveys focus only on new products of given sectors and quickly become outdated.

More importantly, in this course of limited innovation measures, scholars relied on R&D-intensive high-tech industries. This tendency is obvious in the first two measures, R&D expenditure and industry, but it also applies to the studies that examined patents and innovation surveys. The electrical, computer, and semiconductor manufacturing firms are the dominant players in the patent world (see Table 2.2), while broader information technology firms such as Microsoft and Google have been more active in recent years. Moreover, the dominant practice in the pharmaceutical industry is to research new drugs, file patents, mass-produce, and price in a monopolistic way. These are the sectors considered the standard "high-tech" industries (Saxenian 1999; Hecker 2005; DeVol et al. 2009). The SBA's Innovation Database was specifically based on publications focused on the electrical and computer sectors. Thus, discussion of the past innovation studies was primarily about high-tech or so-called "knowledge-intensive" sectors.

Some scholars were aware of these overlapping and somewhat confused boundaries between innovations and high-tech sectors. However, the acknowledgement of this bias and of correlations

Table 2.2   Top 10 US patent granted organizations: 1985–2014

#	1985	1995	2005	2014
1	General Electric	IBM	IBM	IBM
2	Hitachi	Canon	Hitachi	Samsung
3	Toshiba	Motorola	Canon	Canon
4	IBM	NEC	Panasonic	Sony
5	Philips	Mitsubishi Electric	Hewlett-Packard	Microsoft
6	RCA	Toshiba	Samsung	Google
7	Canon	Hitachi	Micron	Toshiba
8	Siemens	Panasonic	Intel	Qualcomm
9	AT&T	Eastman Kodak	Siemens	Panasonic
10	Fuji Photo Film	General Electric	Toshiba	General Electric

Source: USPTO 1985, 1995, 2005, 2014.

between the two have largely remained at the footnote level (Feldman and Florida 1994; Audretsch and Feldman 1996; Acs et al. 2002). Alternately, scholars have used them as a justification for examining the high-tech or knowledge-intensive industries. For instance, the limitations of patents in not measuring non-patented innovations and having no commercial value were underscored by the fact that the regression results with patents and other knowledge-intensive R&D activities were identical (Acs et al. 1994a; Feldman 1999; Varga 1999; Motoyama et al. 2014). Nonetheless, these identical results indeed demonstrate the blurring of innovation inputs and outputs, and the confusion surrounding the means of producing innovations.

This synonymy of innovations and "high-tech" indeed goes back several decades, and Peter Drucker was perhaps the earliest scholar to point it out:

> "Ah," everybody will say immediately, "high tech." But things are not quite that simple. Of the 40 million-plus jobs created since 1965 in the economy, high technology did not contribute more than 5 or 6 million. High tech thus contributed no more than "smokestack" lost. All the additional jobs in the economy were generated elsewhere. And only one or two out of every hundred new businesses – a total of ten thousand a year – are remotely "high-tech," even in the loosest sense of the term. (Drucker 1985, page unknown)

Nonetheless, this synonymy of innovations and "high-tech" has taken over the theoretical debate about the causal mechanism for generating innovations. Even a well-cited article[3] in the knowledge spillover study argued this:

> [I]nnovation in the late twentieth century is unusually dependent on an area's underlying technological infrastructure. Having burst beyond the confines of the organizational boundaries of an individual firm, innovation is increasingly dependent on a geographically defined infrastructure that is capable of mobilizing technical resources, knowledge, and other inputs essential to the innovation process. . . . [And such technological infrastructure] is defined in terms of the agglomeration of four indicators: 1) firms in related industries; 2) university R&D; 3) industrial R&D; and 4) business-service firms. (Feldman and Florida 1994, 210)

Here, the "technological infrastructure" was supposed to be inputs of innovations, but the scholars measured such inputs by further inputs of R&D activities. At the same time, no innovation outputs are empirically measured, but assumed that the series of those innovation inputs were able to produce outputs. This logic creates a misconception of inputs and outputs, as well as the causal mechanism between them, while continuously missing concrete measures of innovation outputs.

2.6 ENTREPRENEURSHIP AS THE OUTPUT AND PROCESS

Given these shortcomings of measuring innovation, we have a limited understanding about the theory and mechanism to produce innovation. In other words, we understand that innovation is important for economic development, but we know little beyond that R&D, patents, and high-tech industries are correlated.

In this book, instead, we propose entrepreneurship as an alternative output measure and an analysis of the economic development mechanism. Entrepreneurship is theoretically considered to be two sides of the same coin with respect to innovations as discussed by Schumpeter: Entrepreneurs are the people who create innovations. However, Schumpeter's framework of entrepreneurs was too broad to include both people who start new companies and those who

---

[3]   As of October 2018, Google Scholars mentions that the Feldman and Florida (1994) article was cited 2,810 times.

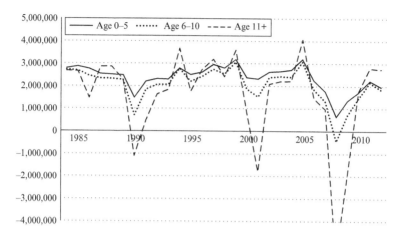

Source: Business Dynamics Statistics, Census Bureau (2016).

Figure 2.1 Net job creation by firm age in the U.S.

create new products at existing and large companies. In this book, we focus on the former, people who start new companies, for an empirical reason.

Recent advancement in large-scale microdata analysis revealed that startup companies are the net job creators in the U.S. (Haltiwanger 2012; Haltiwanger et al. 2013). As Figure 2.1 demonstrates, new and young firms (age zero to five, a solid line) have been the net job creators for the past several decades. On the other hand, companies six to ten years old (a dotted line) are generally net job losers, and companies eleven years or older (a dashed line) have a highly cyclical pattern in which they generate more jobs during good years, but destroy substantial numbers of jobs during recession years. Note that these figures are the 'net' job creation. It is a natural dynamic that young companies create new jobs but lose jobs at the same time. However, the net figure is the sum of job creation and job destruction, which demonstrates that new and young companies are the true job creators, contrary to the conventional wisdom that large (and old) companies are. In this sense, this is a different debate than the one originated by Birch in the 1980s (1981, 1987), in which scholars discussed only the stock of employment level (not the flow of net job creation) between small and large companies (not by the firm age).

This positive effect of entrepreneurship on the economy applies to broader economic aspects such as the growth of GDP and labor productivity, and to other OECD countries such as Germany (Fritsch and Mueller 2008), the UK (Mueller et al. 2008), the Netherlands (Van Stel and Suddle 2008), and another case in the U.S. (Acs and Mueller 2008).

There have been a number of economics and management studies about entrepreneurship, but those earlier studies focused on the microeconomic perspective and examined individual characteristics and behaviors of entrepreneurs (Van de Ven 1993), such as who became entrepreneurs; what kind of individual traits led them to business success; and what kind of skills, experiences, or backgrounds venture capitals look for in entrepreneurs. At the same time, scholars have known that entrepreneurship is largely a local phenomenon (Malecki 1993; Feldman 2003). Silicon Valley is the most well-known example, with its distinguished regional structure and culture where many corporate and university spin-offs are generated, and where entrepreneurs themselves and venture capitalists interact through extensive networks (Saxenian 1994; Kenney 2000; Lecuyer 2006).

Nonetheless, the mainstream studies that concern local economic development studies, such as the agglomeration theories (Marshall 1898; Castells 1989) or industrial cluster theory (Porter 1994, 1998), touched on some notions of entrepreneurship, but it was as one of the peripheral and external factors behind innovation. In other words, they discussed innovation or industry development and observed a high level of entrepreneurship when a region was experiencing high growth in innovation or industrial development. There has been limited discussion about why the level of entrepreneurship was high or how such an entrepreneurship level led to the production of innovation or industry development.

The major reason for this limited attention stems from the difficulty of entrepreneurship in operationalization, as in innovation studies. We revisit this issue in Chapter 3 and examine various data of entrepreneurship. Here, we highlight a few advancements in our understanding of entrepreneurship and regional development.

Chinitz was the first to challenge the then-implicit assumption by regional economists "that the supply schedule of entrepreneurship is identical at all locations" (1961, 284). He analyzed the regional industrial structure associated with entrepreneurial culture and argued that the capital-intensive and oligopolistic steel industry suppressed entrepreneurship and innovation in Pittsburgh, while an economy based on more diverse industries, and the small establishment nature of apparel industry, led to long-term economic development in New York City. This influential work sparked further analyses of the region's average firm size (Evans 1986; Norton 1992; Drucker and Feser 2012) and the diversity of regional industries (Henderson 1986, 2003; Glaeser et al. 1992). However, their focus was on how these regional industrial structures affected the aggregate regional growth, and neglected the role of entrepreneurship underneath.

Several other econometric works have analyzed the regional factors associated with the higher rates of entrepreneurship. Reynolds (1994) found that 1) demand factors, such as population growth and income level or purchasing power, 2) unemployment, and 3) the ratio of small businesses were related to high rates of entrepreneurship. Audretsch and Fritsch (1994) found that the share of unskilled workers was negatively correlated with entrepreneurship rates, which may imply, though not empirically modeled, the correlation between skilled workers and entrepreneurship rates. In addition, Davidsson et al. (1994) found a similar link with the presence of small firms and the proportion employed in technical professions.[4] Acs and Armington (2006) similarly concluded that high entrepreneurship rates correlated with higher rates of college and high school education, population and income growth, a smaller presence of large incumbent firms, and a higher degree of industrial specialization. The major limitation of their studies was the lack of research-related factors in their models. While their theoretical basis was the knowledge spillover theory, they did not incorporate various data on R&D, government, or venture capital funding because their primary data source was labor and industry data. Yet they considered those knowledge spillover indicators to be represented by the highly correlated variable, the share of college-educated adults (Acs and Armington 2006, 64). Acs et al. (2009) then conducted inter-country analyses of entrepreneurship rates by incorporating some R&D-related data, such as patents and R&D expenditure over GDP, and concluded with the positive roles of human capital and R&D activities.

---

[4] There was a special issue of *Regional Studies* dedicated to the analysis of regional factors associated with entrepreneurship rates, and their findings were insightful. Many of those findings became the basis of knowledge spillover theory in entrepreneurship by Acs and Audretsch.

There has been a new wave of so-called entrepreneurship "ecosystem" studies from the geography and management fields since the 2000s. Earlier studies primarily examined what elements constituted a local entrepreneurship ecosystem. Feldman (2001) identified that pioneering entrepreneurs, supportive social capital, venture capital, entrepreneurial support services, and engaged research universities were essential to form an entrepreneurial culture in the Washington DC area. According to Neck et al. (2004) and Cohen (2006), those elements were incubators, spin-off firms, formal and informal networks, physical infrastructure, and culture. Isenberg (2011) similarly argued that finance, support, human capital, markets, policy, and culture were essential elements.

There are three major limitations of these past ecosystem studies. First, many of the identified elements are remarkably similar to the list of elements in the cluster theory by Porter (1994, 1998, 2000): rival firms, a labor force, risk capital (such as venture capitals), specialized support services, research universities, and corporate labs. Thus, what the ecosystem studies examined may be a replacement of industrial cluster, also inheriting the limitation of the cluster studies with its inability to explain connections between these elements (Martin and Sunley 2003; Motoyama 2008). Second, there is apparently confusion between elements of a system, which should be actors, such as individuals and firms, and features of a system, which may be an aggregate behavior of or between elements, such as social capital, culture, and supportive attitude. Such confusion does not help to explain how the system works. Moreover, that your region needs a culture to support entrepreneurship or a risk-taking attitude is impractical. Third and most importantly, discussing the presence of elements (actors and organizations) does not warrant an effective function of a system. Virtually all large urban areas have the elements listed above, yet some function better than others. For instance, Baltimore is the home of the Johns Hopkins University medical school, and its annual research expenditure of over $2 billion dwarfs that of Harvard, Stanford, and MIT combined (Carnegie Commission on Higher Education 2013). The State of Maryland aggressively promoted innovation and entrepreneurship, and established incubators and venture funds. Nonetheless, entrepreneurship rates and economic development in the region is dismal, and clearly the system is not working (Feldman and Desrochers 2003, 2004). Similarly, Cleveland should enjoy benefits of research-intensive universities, such as Case Western and Cleveland State, as well as a major research center of the National Institute of Standards and Technology (NIST), but those do not turn into economic outputs (Fogarty and Sinha 1999). Breznitz and Taylor criticized the elements-focused framework and proposed that we need to pursue a structure-focused approach in which they analyzed "the structure of the relationship among agents, be they firms, individuals, associations or governments within the cluster" (2014, 376).

Other and more recent entrepreneurship ecosystem studies advanced some understandings about the local system of entrepreneurship. For example, Malecki (1993, 2009) discussed the importance of entrepreneurial culture, including support organizations, as well as the presence and acknowledgment of role model entrepreneurs in nearby families and at the regional level. Spigel (2016, 2017) more holistically defined that a local entrepreneurship system was configured through the combination of 1) the socially based networks, 2) the "material" attributes like universities, other institutions, and policies that create publicly funded support programs, and 3) the cultural attributes, such as attitudes toward entrepreneurship, and industrial and entrepreneurial history within a region. However, these culture-oriented studies tried to capture local systems even more broadly, thus limiting the capacity to analyze how entrepreneurs interact with each other within a local setting.

In the meantime, other studies shifted analysis on the roles of high-growth companies instead of startup companies (NESTA 2009; OECD 2010). Bos and Stam (2013) examined geography of young high-growth firms in the Netherlands, and Motoyama (2015), Li et al. (2016), and Rice et al. (2017) did so in the USA. Brown and Mawson (2016) found that high-growth firms in Scotland aggressively acquired firms internationally. All those studies agreed that high-growth firms existed in every major city and even in some rural places. Thus, the geography of high-growth firms is not limited to global cities, like London or Silicon Valley, and venture capitals or research universities are not a prerequisite for firm growth (Brown et al. 2017).

In sum, we are starting to understand that entrepreneurial activities depend on more than the "stock of knowledge" productions represented in a) research activities and funding and b) human capital, as discussed by the knowledge spillover theory. The aggregate stock of knowledge expressed at the regional level may correlate with many other factors, but the correlation itself does not explain how people, specifically entrepreneurs, behave within the regional system. There are important macroeconomic environments that affect the performance and success of firms in a given region. However, culture is not just inputs, but also outcomes of how individuals behave, and often this evolves in the regional context. Thus, we still have limited understanding about the functions of such local entrepreneurship systems, and the roles of entrepreneurs still remains largely a black box (Stam 2015). This subfield is undertheorized and underdeveloped (Brown and Mason 2017; Spigel and Harrison 2018; Stam and Spigel 2018).

In this book, we investigate this subject with multiple methods and in-depth regional case studies. Our primary examination is about entrepreneurs because it is about local systems for entrepreneurship, and entrepreneurs are the core of the systems. This requires a microeconomic analysis of entrepreneurs at the individual level. In addition, we pay close attention to the interactions of individual actors to mesolevel organizations and networks within a region, as well as macroeconomic features and expectations that affect the behavior of individuals; what Douglas North called institutions (1987, 1990).

In Chapter 3, we examine quantitative aspects of entrepreneurship and the difference between innovation factors at the national scale. We start with an assumption that entrepreneurship may require different sets of inputs.

3. What does the nationwide data say?

3.1 MEASURES OF ENTREPRENEURSHIP

It is relatively easy to qualitatively conceptualize entrepreneurship as an act of starting a new company and a successful growth of it. In this book, we base the role of entrepreneurship in economic development as the net job creator, and Chapter 2 demonstrated that it is the new and young companies (zero to five years old) that contribute to this job creation. However, this qualitative scope is extremely difficult to capture quantitatively. There have been varieties of data on entrepreneurship; however, each set of data comes with pros and cons. The purpose of this section is to review these varied data, propose a new set for this book, and analyze the regional factors for high entrepreneurship.

The first type of entrepreneurship data, primarily collected by the Census Bureau, is self-employment. This has an extremely broad scope of entrepreneurship by including people who own companies of just themselves (incorporated), people who do not even technically own a company but get paid in various ways (unincorporated), people who hire a few employees, or people who hire even a few thousand employees. According to the American Community Survey (Census Bureau 2014), 6.4 percent of the American population is classified as self-employed. There are two limitations to this data. First, the category does not demonstrate anything about the creation of a new company (flow), but rather the state of employer/employee status (stock). Second, as it captures any person owning a business or getting paid as an independent contractor, even with no employee and no growth, it overlaps more with small businesses.

Fairlie et al. (2015) improved this data by applying the rotating sample in the Current Population Survey and analyzed the ratio of "new" entrepreneurs by identifying people who are not self-employed in the first survey, but who are self-employed in the second survey. According to this estimate, the newly self-employed people consisted of 0.31 percent of the population. This indicator was an improvement from the stock of self-employment, but it still captured all kinds of incorporated or unincorporated and employer or non-employer businesses.

The second type of entrepreneurship data is establishment-based. Here, an establishment is different from a firm: A firm is a company that operates under one organization. An establishment is a branch of a firm. In that sense, an establishment-based data has limitations to measure the state of new firm creation. The simplest form of this data by the past studies is the establishment per capita or average firm size (Acs and Armington 2003; Acs and Mueller 2008; Lee, Florida, and Acs 2004; Mueller 2007). In theory, this ratio should explain whether a region is dominated by a few large companies – thus a smaller establishment per capita – or consists of many small companies – thus a larger establishment per capita. There are two major limitations to this approach. First, this may reflect the industrial structure of a given region rather than its state of entrepreneurship. In other words, a remote town with an automobile factory will have a low establishment per capita and look less entrepreneurial than a tourism town with many restaurants and hotels. Second, the establishment ratio as the stock does not necessarily represent entrepreneurship because entrepreneurship is about the dynamism of economy, and it will be more important to include the flow data about new establishments.

There have been some efforts to measure the flow information with new firm establishments. Low and Isserman (2015) developed multiple filters to improve the measure. First, they selected innovative industries by calculating the higher ratio of "high-tech occupations" defined by the Bureau of Labor Statistics (Feser 2003; Hecker 2005), intensity of patents, and industry churn. The results produced 36 "innovative entrepreneurship" sectors (Low and Isserman 2015, 177) at the three-digit North American Industry Classification System (NAICS) level. Second, they analyzed the birth rate of single-unit non-employer and employer establishments. Then, they demonstrated that their measures were statistically different from other entrepreneurship rates such as self-employment, proprietorship, or small businesses.

Acs and Armington (2006) conducted a pioneering work based on the Longitudinal Establishment and Enterprise Microdata (LEEM), which covered every business establishment in the U.S. with any tax return and payroll filings, that is, businesses that hired employees.

3.2 ENTREPRENEURSHIP MEASURES IN THIS BOOK

In this chapter, we follow the approach to measuring new firm creation of Low and Isserman (2015) and Acs and Armington (2006). However, we extend it to capture more dimensions of entrepreneurship by proposing three sets of dependent variables. The first measure is the rate of new firm creation in all industries based on the Business Dynamics Statistics (BDS) of the Census Bureau. This BDS data is generated from the Longitudinal Business Database (LBD), essentially the same data source as the LEEM used by Acs and Armington (2006), and constructed by linking data files from the Census Bureau's Business Register (2013). This data focuses on employer firms, thus filtering out self-employment and better capturing firms that grow and employ people, the essential component of entrepreneurship. We use the metropolitan areas as the unit of analysis.

The darker colors in Figure 3.1 represent higher entrepreneurship rates, and many of the darkest fall in the Sunbelt areas such as in Florida, Texas, Southern California, and Arizona. However, there are other high-activity areas in New York City and other central parts of the U.S. such as Salt Lake City-Provo, Denver-Boulder, and St. Louis. Contrary to the perception, Silicon Valley does not enjoy the highest level of startup activities.

The second measure is the rate of new firm creation in selected high-tech industries based on National Establishment Time-Series (NETS) data. As we reviewed in Chapter 2, the high-tech sectors received the lion's share of investigation in innovation studies, and here we test the new firm creation rate for the high-tech sectors. The BDS data is reliable with its comprehensive coverage of employer firms, but it does not provide industry breakdown for high-tech sectors with the two-digit NAICS code level. Instead, we use NETS data which provide detailed industry information at the establishment and firm level.

This data is originally collected by Dun and Bradstreet and converted to time-series data by Walls and Associates. They collect

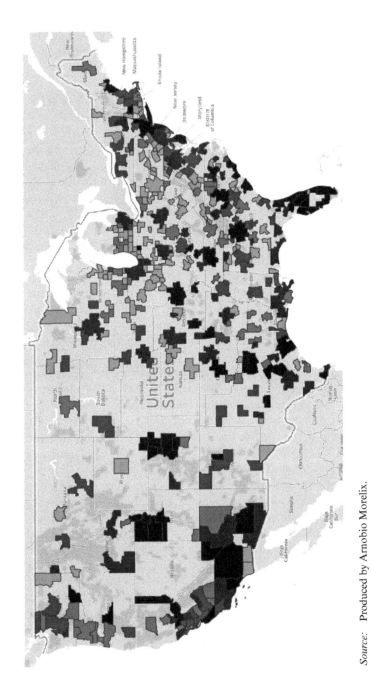

Source: Produced by Arnobio Morelix.

Figure 3.1 Map of BDS startup rate in all industries

data from public and private businesses, including employer firms and the self-employed, sole proprietors, nonprofits, and government establishments. We can systematically exclude nonprofit and government establishments based on industry, but the limitation of this data is that it includes non-employer firms, such as self-employment and sole proprietorship. We follow the high-tech definition provided by the Bureau of Labor Statistics (Hecker 2005), and the special tabulation of the new firm rate provided by Hathaway (2013). The high-tech sectors essentially include the information and communication, pharmaceutical, aerospace, engineering services, and scientific research and development sectors.

With the second measure, the usual tech-hubs (Chapple et al. 2004) seem to overlap as shown in Figure 3.2: Seattle, Portland-Corvallis, San Francisco Bay Area, and Washington, DC. At the same time, there are other high startup activities within high-tech sectors in the center, such as Chicago, Minneapolis, Kansas City, and again Denver-Boulder and Salt Lake City-Provo.

The third measure of entrepreneurship in this chapter is the "Inc. 5000" firms. Every year, *Inc.* magazine ranks the fast-growing private firms with more than $2 million in annual revenue, based on revenue growth in the previous three years. We find a range of growth rates on the list, so further apply the high-growth definition used by the Organisation for Economic Co-operation and Development (OECD 2010): more than 20 percent revenue growth for three consecutive years or 72.8 percent growth over three years. We find between 2,700 and 2,800 firms per year in this category, and call them the *Inc.* high-growth firms. In recent years, there has been some geographic analysis of *Inc.* firms at the state level (Motoyama 2015) or the county level (Li et al. 2016). This chapter analyzes at the metropolitan level and compares the results with other startup indicators of entrepreneurship.

With the third measure, the areas on the East Coast are highlighted: Boston and all the metro areas between New York City, Washington, DC, and Atlanta (see Figure 3.3). In the middle part of the country, the dark areas fall into Minneapolis and, again, Denver-Boulder, Austin, and Salt Lake City-Provo. The San Francisco Bay Area is also high.

We draw independent variables primarily from the knowledge spillover literature (Jaffe et al. 1993; Feldman and Florida 1994; Audretsch and Feldman 1996, 2004; and Feldman and Audretsch

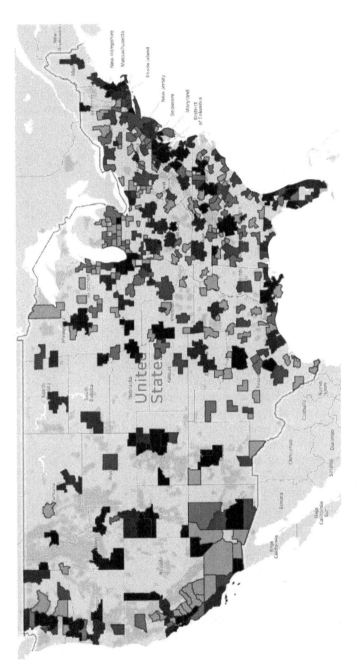

Source: Produced by Arnobio Morelix.

Figure 3.2 Map of NETS startup rate in high-tech sectors

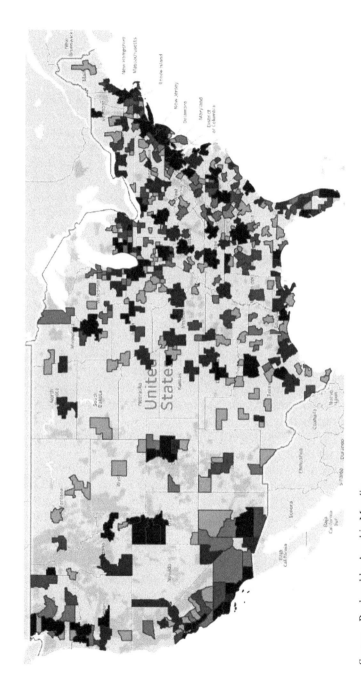

Source: Produced by Arnobio Morelix.

Figure 3.3   Map of the Inc. *high-growth firm ratio*

1999). These studies identified that innovation is a function of university research, industrial research, presence of related businesses (that is, the industrial cluster), and human capital. For university research, we measure the number of so-called Research I universities in a region using the Carnegie Classification.[1] For government research, we include the funding level of Small Business Innovation Research or National Institutes of Health (NIH) normalized by the population size. For industrial research, research expenditure by the private sector will be the most relevant measure. However, we want to control for the presence of high-tech sectors, which by definition are the industries with high-level research activities. Since we cannot include these two variables in the same model, we only use the Location Quotient (LQ) of high-tech sectors provided by the Milken Institute (DeVol et al. 2009).

While the level of patent production was the dependent variable of knowledge spillover, we treat it as the independent variable. We control for the population size and growth rate. Note that the second wave of knowledge spillover studies (Acs and Armington 2003, 2006) used entrepreneurship rates as the dependent variable and included the human capital factor as independent variables, but did not incorporate research and development activities in their regression models due to data unavailability and assumed those R&D activities are reflected in the human capital factor. Thus, we will pay specific attention to those research factors once we control for human capital and patent production.

Since Reynolds (1994) identified the correlation of entrepreneurship rates with purchasing power, we include the regional average of household income. Moreover, two studies observed the influence of migration factor (Audretsch and Fritsch 1994; Keeble and Walker 1994), so we include the population flux, that is, the rate of in- and out-migration over total population. Following the finding of industrial specialization by Acs and Armington (2006), we introduce an index of economic diversity by counting the number of industries over a Location Quotient of 1.1 based on the Woods and Pools Index. This variable ranges from one for a metro with no industrial specialization to six for the New York metro. See Appendix Table A.2 for descriptive statistics.

---

[1]   There are 108 very high research activity universities under Category 15.

There are currently 366 metropolitan areas defined by the Office of Management and Budget (OMB). We follow the 2009 definition of metropolitan areas to be compatible with the BDS. Lastly, we include nine regional dummies of Census divisions: Northeast, Mid-Atlantic, East Midwest, West Midwest, South Atlantic, East South Central, West South Central, Mountain, and Pacific. East Midwest served as the base case: Illinois, Indiana, Michigan, Ohio, and Wisconsin.

3.3 REGRESSION ANALYSIS[2]

This is a technical section, and non-technical audiences may prefer to skip to section 3.4. The distribution of each of the three dependent variables is different, so we apply different regression techniques.

First, the BDS data is slightly skewed to the right, but OLS can still robustly explain it. Second, the NETS data are highly skewed to the right, so we employ a log form. Third, the *Inc.* data are similarly skewed to the right with 106 zero value, so we add one to this variable and employ a log form.

As shown in Table 3.1, all three models are statistically significant, and the adjusted R-square ranges from 0.45 to 0.74, meaning that each model can explain 45 percent to 74 percent of variation. This is high considering we only have twelve factors to explain in addition to eight regional dummy variables.

We examine the result of each model and review the three models together. First, for startup activities of all industries, the population size, growth, and flux are statistically significant and positive. In other words, the larger the metro population, its growth, and flows of people are, the more startups are found. The average household income or economic diversity is not significant. Neither is the LQ of high-tech sectors, which suggests that the presence of high-tech industry per se does not spill over to all the other sectors. The college or high school completion rates are insignificant, so the general level of human capital is not correlated with startup activities of this type. Importantly, many of the research factors are insignificant: Research I, SBIR, and patents per capita. The only significant factor

[2] I would like to thank Emil Malizia for analyses I employed in this section which I learned through our past projects (Malizia and Motoyama 2016, 2019; Motoyama and Malizia 2017).

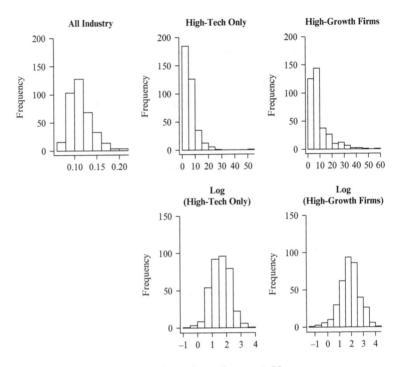

Figure 3.4   Histogram of three dependent variables

is investment by venture capitals (VC). Metros in the Mountain and South Atlantic regions have higher level of startup activities.

Second, for startup activities of high-tech sectors, we find similar results with a few caveats. All the population-related factors are similarly significant, and now the average household income is also important. Economic diversity and the stock of patents are insignificant, but the presence of high-tech sectors is significant. Thus, high-tech clusters are associated with high-tech startups. While the high school completion rate is still unimportant, now the college completion rate is significant. That is, areas with high-tech sector startups co-exist with well-educated labor. SBIR is now significant, but VC-like investment is not. Again, patents have no correlation. Unexpectedly, Research I universities are statistically significant and negative, meaning that the presence of research-intensive universities is associated with lower levels of high-tech startups.

Third, the high-growth firm model is more or less similar to the

Table 3.1   Regression results

Variables	All industry		High-tech only		Inc high-growth	
	Coeff.	Sig.	Coeff.	Sig.	Coeff.	Sig.
(Intercept)	−0.0625		−2.2440	***	9.8340	***
log10(Pop)	0.0249	***	0.3033	***	1.7280	***
Pop growth	0.2200	***	2.1480	***	2.1130	**
Ave. HH income	0.0000		0.0000	***	0.0000	
Pop flux	0.0875	**	1.3100	**	−0.1226	
Econ diversity	0.0001		−0.0041		0.0007	
Tech.LQ	−0.0022		0.1862	***	0.2611	
Patents per 100K	0.0000		0.0003		−0.0001	
Research I univ	0.0008		−0.0804	**	−0.0138	
SBIR per cap	0.0000		0.0033	**	0.0045	**
Investment	0.0000	***	0.0000		0.0000	
College completion	−0.0003		0.0223	***	0.0166	***
High school completion	0.0002		0.0097		0.0073	
region (East South Central)	0.0048		0.1038		0.1172	
region (Mid-Atlantic)	0.0036		−0.0747		−0.1812	
region (Mountain)	0.0209	***	0.5040	***	0.0392	
region (Northeast)	0.0095		0.0793		−0.0169	
region (Pacific)	0.0051		0.1105		−0.0501	
region (South Atlantic)	0.0146	***	0.2031	***	0.0226	
region (West Midwest)	0.0053		0.0370		−0.0470	
region (West South Central)	0.0077		0.0141		−0.1586	
DF	345		345		345	
F-stats	16.050		37.890		53.590	
Adj. R-sq	0.452		0.669		0.742	

Note: *** means the significance at the 99 percent level; ** at the 95 percent level.

high-tech startup model. The population size and growth are significant, but population flux and average household income are not. The college completion rate is significant, but the presence of a high-tech cluster is not. Again, all the research factors are insignificant except the funding of SBIR.

3.4 DISCUSSION

The regression results of the three models demonstrate critical differences with the knowledge spillover theory. First and foremost, most research factors are not correlated to entrepreneurship factors. The stock of patents is not correlated in all the models. Note that the knowledge spillover theory suggested that the level of innovation measured by patents was correlated with research-related factors. Once the patent level is controlled, the patent and most other research factors are not correlated with entrepreneurship activities.

The number of Research I universities is not significant, and their presence is even negative in the high-tech model. This is perplexing, but it is possible that some research universities are located in small towns with few commercial and high-tech activities; for example, University of Illinois at Urbana-Champaign and Cornell University at Ithaca, New York (Patton and Kenney 2010). To exclude small college towns, we test our model only with 102 metropolitan areas with populations greater than 500,000.[3] The results are the same except that the negative coefficient of Research I is no longer statistically significant at the 95 percent level. Thus, Research I universities do not seem to be a negative factor for large metropolitan areas. We additionally test this factor by broadening 1) the number of universities to include 99 high research activity universities and 90 doctoral research universities (under categories16 and 17 of the Carnegie Classification, respectively), and 2) the scope of research activities with the number of full-time faculty, full-time researchers, undergraduate and graduate students, and research expenditure. None of these factors are statistically significant in all models. It seems safe to conclude that the presence of research universities or their research activities are unrelated to regional entrepreneurial activities.

Since some NIH funds are distributed through SBIR, we cannot include these two variables in the same model. Then, we also test by substituting SBIR funding with NIH funding, and find that NIH is insignificant in all models. At least, SBIR is significant in the high-tech and high-growth models. This indicates that not all government research funds are uncorrelated with entrepreneurship activities, but only some are. Investment by VC or other private equity is sporadi-

---

[3] We use this cut-off point of 500,000 inhabitants by following the definition of college towns by Qian and Yao (2017).

cally significant, only in the all-industry model. This is not an intuitive finding because VCs are known to invest in high-tech sectors and high-growth companies (PricewaterhouseCoopers 2011, 2015), and we do not have a good explanation. At minimum, our finding indicates that where there is high startup activity at the all-industry level, there is a high level of VC-type investment. We revisit this issue in Chapter 5, analysis on high-growth firms, and Chapter 7, the conclusion.

The part where our models agree with the knowledge spillover theory is the importance of human capital. We do not find a correlation with the high school completion rate, but the college completion rate is significant in high-tech and high-growth models. Together with the insignificance in the all-industry model, we interpret it as the need for higher skills to launch startups in high-tech sectors or high-growth firms, but not for startups in all industries.

Some works under the knowledge spillover theory took steps to further test the relations with more detailed human capital factors. For instance, Audretsch and Fritsch (1994) found that the share of unskilled workers was negatively correlated with entrepreneurship rates, which may imply, though not empirically modeled, the correlation between skilled workers and entrepreneurship rates. In addition, Davidsson et al. (1994) found a similar link with the presence of small firms and the proportion employed in technical professions. However, we must be cautious here because the measure on those types of workers or occupations is highly correlated with income and education levels. Keeble and Walker (1994, 418) cautioned this multicollinearity, but it is unacknowledged in later knowledge spillover studies (Acs and Storey 2004; Acs et al. 2009; Acs et al. 2013). This is a complicated issue with quantitative modeling, and there is no easy solution. Having said that, we revisit this human capital issue in Chapter 5 where in-depth interviews of entrepreneurs uncover what kind of human capital is needed in high-growth companies.

In addition, the demand factor, the sheer size of population and its growth, is associated with entrepreneurial activities. The significance of both simply means that you find more entrepreneurship activities where more people live and grow. While this is an intuitive finding, it indicates the potential dichotomy between regions: Growing regions grow more, while others do not. Such a pattern of regional divergence echoes other empirical studies (Ó hUallacháin 1999; Bettencourt et al. 2007; Motoyama et al. 2014), and implies the difficulty in changing the course of entrepreneurship activities.

Moreover, the significance of population flux in the all-industry and high-tech models is noteworthy. As discussed above, we already control for the population growth, yet the population flux measure of both in- and outflow is correlated with higher startup activities. Thus, it means that places not only with higher growth, but also with higher flow of people have a higher level of entrepreneurship. As a reference, the statistical correlation between population growth and flux is relatively low, 0.31, so there are many regions with little population growth but with high population flux, or regions with little population flux but with high population growth. Taken together, regions with little population growth and low flow of people suffer from low rates of startup activities.

These findings open up a new debate about important factors for entrepreneurship activities. With our models of explicit entrepreneurship measures as the dependent variables, much of the core group of knowledge spillover factors is unrelated to entrepreneurship. We have to keep in mind that these cross-sectional regressions do not demonstrate causality, but only indicate statistical associations between the dependent and independent variables. However, statistical insignificance or disassociation is a powerful finding. It effectively demonstrates that some factors do not have any linkage to various entrepreneurial activities, in this case previously assumed research and patent activities. A region may have a high level of technologies in patents or at research universities, but they do not necessarily spill over to entrepreneurship activities. You may further add VC investment or government funding, such as NIH, but they do not correlate with entrepreneurship, either. Specific forms of government funding, such as SBIR, are associated with entrepreneurship, and we need to investigate further.

Moreover, regional clusters of high-tech sectors do not translate into entrepreneurship activities of other sectors or high-growth firms except the startup activity of the high-tech sectors themselves. Thus, being high-tech does not drive the economy through entrepreneurship. The high-tech sectors constituted only 10.5 percent of non-farm wage jobs in 2012, and their employment growth has been slower than the rest of economy since 1992 (Hecker 2005). At the same time, the statistical significance of the high-tech LQ indicates some form of sector-based spillover.

We have found significance in some forms of human capital factors. While the population size and growth provide few policy implications, the education level and population flux provide hints, as well as inquiries, about how highly educated people interact within a region and move between organizations and regions.

The analysis in this chapter was essentially about what regional factors are associated with higher rates of entrepreneurship, and this was a "30,000-feet" analysis. We have negated several factors and found some clues about potentially effective factors. While regressions provide the breadth of coverage at the national scale, such highly aggregated regional data are not the best tools to explore how the effective factors are organized within the region, especially around the human-based activities.

For the next two chapters, we shift our analysis to explore those dimensions of human capital at a deeper and ground level. It is critical to investigate cases outside Silicon Valley and Boston, the two areas on which the currently dominant innovation theories have relied. Here, we follow the framework of the "second-tier cities" by Markusen and colleagues (1999) and Mayer (2011) by highlighting spatially distinct areas of economic activities with high growth in population and technology-intensive industries. We conduct in-depth case studies of the Kansas City and St. Louis metropolitan areas. Each area hosts at least one so-called Carnegie Research I university and has a presence of major high-tech firms. Therefore, each – theoretically – has the right assets for innovation and entrepreneurship activities, and connections between universities and industries. We examine how entrepreneurs get ideas and behave within these environments.

The entrepreneurial activity of these two regions is noteworthy as they have experienced a major surge in entrepreneurship activities in recent years. Here, we use the same BDS startup rate introduced in this chapter. The startup rate has been generally declining since the 1980s, and the decline in the late 2000s was substantial (Hathaway and Litan 2014). Even as of 2014, the startup rate had recovered marginally in the U.S., while the two regions marked a clear recovery since 2010 (Figure 3.5). The recovery by St. Louis is particularly notable as it surpassed that of San Jose (Silicon Valley), and that of Kansas City surpassed the national rate and became comparable to that of San Jose. This pattern in the regionwide census data demonstrates a clear sign of something going on in these areas with regard to entrepreneurship.

Within these two regions, we will focus on how people, more

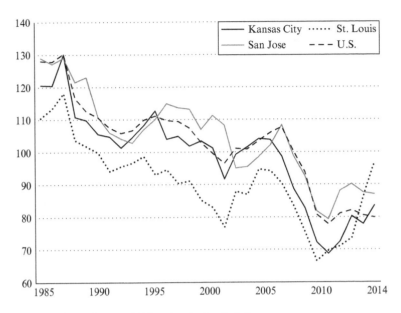

Source: Census Bureau (2016) and author's calculation.

Figure 3.5   Startup rate in three metro areas and the U.S.

specifically entrepreneurs, conduct their entrepreneurial journeys. Our premise is that entrepreneurship is fundamentally driven by human-based activities, not institutionally driven by universities, scientific discoveries, formalized knowledge of specific technologies called patents, or large-scale funding. We need to understand how people, specifically entrepreneurs, get connected, use local resources, and learn from and are influenced by each other. Moreover, such connectivity around entrepreneurs is organized at the regional level.

4. What do entrepreneurs do in the City of Fountains? A case study of Kansas City

4.1 INTRODUCTION AND BACKGROUND

The Kansas City area may be considered one of the ordinary metropolitan areas of Midwest America. Once the 15th-largest metropolitan area in the nation in the 1970s, it also used to be the second-largest automobile assembly outside Detroit (Gibson 1998), and tried to transform its image as an agricultural processing center or an isolated cow town in the dusty plains to "one of the few livable cities left" or "the nation's inland capital" (Bayless 1978). The slogan that emerged then was "more fountains than Rome, more boulevards than Paris" (Barnes 1974; Shortridge 2012).

Despite those efforts, it currently is the 30th-largest US metropolitan area with population of about 2 million, behind Las Vegas (2.1 million) and ahead of Cleveland (also 2 million). It is certainly not the car manufacturing city of Detroit, the commodity trading center of Chicago, the logistical hub of St. Louis, or even the agricultural region of Iowa. The region may be best known for Kansas City barbecue and jazz, and does not present strong industrial characteristics at first glance. There is no industry with a LQ higher than 1.4 at the two-digit NAICS level. The closest are 322 Paper manufacturing (1.37) and 323 Printing (1.36), a cluster related to greeting card manufacturer Hallmark and its suppliers (Motoyama et al. 2013).

However, this ordinary region is home to several global high-tech players, such as Garmin for GPS, Cerner for medical systems, DST for financial security systems, and Sprint for telecommunications. Mayer (2013) reported dozens of spin-outs from these local anchor companies. Little known outside the area, BATS Global Marketing is the third-largest equity exchange trading in the U.S. after the New York Stock Exchange and NASDAQ (BATS 2016). Additionally, there are more than 250 life sciences companies in pharmaceutical development, diagnostic, and clinical research (Kansas City Area Life Sciences Institute 2016), and firms in the region account for 56 percent of the $19 billion worldwide market in animal health, diagnostics, and pet food sales (KC Animal Health Corridor 2016).

Geographically, it is one of the few metropolitan areas where the same name of city exists on both sides of bordering states, Missouri and Kansas, and the metropolitan area is divided more or less equally between those two states. Given that situation, the two states have engaged in a so-called "border war" wherein each state spends millions of dollars annually to steal companies from the other side, and lose those same companies to the other side a few years later (LeRoy 2005).

We should not overlook the presence of several research universities in the area. The University of MissouriKansas City (UMKC) is a high research activity university according to the Carnegie Classification. The University of Kansas (KU) is a very high research activity university located in Lawrence, Kansas, 45 miles west of Kansas City, and the two metropolitan areas are considered as one region with daily commuters from and to both sides. In addition, the University of Kansas has a separate medical center in Kansas City, Kansas, which has 967 full-time staff and spends $67 million per year on research activities. Last but not least, Stowers Institute is an independent center for medical research with 22 principal investigators and 550 staff and over $100 million expenditure per annum (Stowers 2016). In sum, the region has the right assets for innovation activities with globally sourcing high-tech companies and high research institutions. Yet, how entrepreneurship works in this region may be a different story.

The regression results at the metropolitan level from Chapter 3 demonstrated that the entrepreneurship rates did not correlate with the stock of patents or university research, but did with the ratio of highly educated population. In this chapter, we first examine high-tech firms through a survey about their perspectives on whether and how the firms have used patents or university research, as well as what they consider the source of firm growth. The survey data affirms the regression results and reveals a few more specific ways that firms interact with local research universities, including what kind of human capital factors they consider crucial. Second, we focus on entrepreneurs who went through the 1 Million Cups program to deepen our understanding toward the power of peer-based learning and the development of local connections that entrepreneurs go through in their business process.

4.2   SURVEY OF HIGH-TECH FIRMS IN KANSAS CITY[1]

The first kind of data is a survey of high-tech firms in the region. We cast a broad net among information technology and life sciences firms, the two core – generally considered "high-tech" – sectors, and examine what the firms consider their sources of growth. This focus on high-tech sectors is important because, in theory, the R&D-intensive firms in the high-tech sectors should have a closer linkage to university research and a higher use of patents and other forms of intellectual properties. The findings from Chapter 3 based on regressions did not identify correlations between various entrepreneurship rates and these R&D factors, but they were the macroeconomic data at the regional level, and the question was essentially what regional assets were associated with higher rates of entrepreneurship. Here, we examine what firms consider sources for their firm growth, that is, at the microeconomic level.

Since there is no uniform directory or association of those high-tech firms, we distributed the survey through mixed channels with targeted recruitment and a snowballing method. There are limitations with this method, such as the representativeness; however, we leveraged advertising through multiple major channels to minimize a biased sampling from a specific segment of firms: a) the major local media, such as *The Kansas City Star* and the *Kansas City Business Journal*, and b) industry and entrepreneurship support organizations, such as the Greater Kansas City Chamber of Commerce, the Ewing Marion Kauffman Foundation, Kansas City SourceLink, and Think Big Partners, to name a few. We distributed and collected surveys between November 2012 and January 2013.

We obtained 211 valid firms for the analysis of this section,[2]

---

[1]   This section was written with Heike Mayer.

[2]   The original survey contained questions about firm founders and their past entrepreneurial activities, thus including both firms and individuals. The total responses were 568. The valid 211 responses for this section comes after the confirmation of the

Table 4.1   Descriptive statistics of surveyed firms

Employee	Count	Share	Firm age	Count	Share
1–4	112	53.1%	0–1	49	23.2%
5–9	29	13.7%	2–5	69	32.7%
10–99	49	23.2%	6–9	31	14.7%
100+	21	10.0%	10+	62	29.4%

and the firms were well distributed across scale and firm age. The majority (53.1 percent) of firms were very small with one to four employees, but there were firms with 10 to 99 employees (23.2 percent) and 100 or more employees (10.0 percent). The responding firms were relatively young with a median firm age of four. The share of newborn firms (between zero and one year) was 23 percent, and the firms of 10 years or older totaled 29 percent. In general, we oversampled very small and very large firms, as well as very young and older firms, compared to the overall firms in the economy.

The first question for the analysis here is: How important have the following been for your firm's development? From the scale of one to five, the firms rated highly "Informal local access to innovative people and ideas" (mean score 4.15), "Supportive local entrepreneurship organizations" (4.01), and "Attractive local quality of life for staff and management" (3.96). In contrast, the responding firms gave low ratings for research related factors such as "Research links with a university" (2.66), "Quality of local research staff" (2.80), and "Research links with other firms or organizations" (2.82). The fact that the lowest-ranking were for these three research-related factors indicates the strong evidence that firms did not consider research function or connection, at least externally, as the source of firm development, despite the presence of highly research-intensive universities in the region.

The highest-rated factor, "Informal local access to innovative people and ideas," is worth revisiting. It is intuitive to find that companies seek innovative people and ideas. At the same time,

employment and explicit founded year (thus, not just a business idea or in transition between companies, but firms with explicit operation), and the location (thus, excluding firms which used to be located in the Kansas City area, but moved out to other regions). Mayer (2013) reported the result of the founders and spinoff activities.

Table 4.2   Regional advantages

Important factors for firm's development	Mean score	Somewhat or extremely significant
Informal local access to innovative people, ideas	4.15	81.7%
Supportive local entrepreneurship organizations	4.01	72.1%
Attractive local quality of life for staff and management	3.96	77.2%
Access to local business services	3.73	64.5%
Local availability of managerial/professional staff	3.64	57.6%
Access to Midwestern markets	3.48	53.3%
Proximity to local customers	3.38	56.1%
Access to local sources of capital, finance	3.24	45.9%
Supportive local training organizations	3.12	37.5%
Proximity to local suppliers, subcontractors	2.99	35.1%
Local shareholders	2.91	31.5%
Research links with other firms or organizations	2.82	32.0%
Quality of local research staff	2.80	27.9%
Research links with a university	2.66	26.7%

Note: N=211.

firms tended to disassociate innovative people and ideas from local research staff or other research-related factors. Thus, this also signals that innovations may come from something other than research or researchers.

We have asked a similar question by highlighting regional constraints: How significant or insignificant have the following constraints been for your firm's development? First, the firms rated that finance (mean score 3.17), technology talent (3.10), marketing and sales talent (2.67), and management talent (2.55) were the top concerns. Thus, for firm development, the shortage of talent in various forms is a critical issue. On the other hand, the shortage of local research talent (2.43) is considered a lower constraint, and similarly, world-class university (2.26) was not identified as a major constraint for firm development. Other low-ranked constraints include lack of subcontractors (2.39) or suppliers (2.11). Note that the mean score for regional constraints is significantly lower than that of regional advantages for firm growth, meaning that firms overall consider that the region offers many advantageous assets for firm growth.

Table 4.3   Regional constraints

Constraining factors	Mean score	Somewhat or extremely important
Difficulty in accessing local sources of capital, finance	3.17	45.1%
Shortage of local technology talent	3.10	41.8%
Shortage of local marketing and sales talent	2.67	25.3%
Lack of a local market/customers	2.66	24.0%
Shortage of local management talent	2.55	21.2%
Inadequate local business services	2.54	17.1%
Lack of local networking with other firms in the same industry	2.47	20.8%
Shortage of local research talent	2.43	14.4%
Lack of local subcontractors	2.39	17.0%
Lack of world-class university	2.26	15.0%
Lack of appropriate premises (facilities, offices, etc.) locally	2.17	14.2%
Lack of local suppliers	2.11	8.3%

Note: N=211.

Additionally, we asked a similar question about the source of new ideas: Where do your new ideas come from? Though the sample here (162) is smaller than the previous questions (211), the answers are consistent with the important regional factors for firms' development. Mentors (52.5 percent), customers (43.8 percent), and informal networks (42 percent) are the most important sources. Lagging behind, internal R&D units are the next source (33.3 percent), which suggests the importance of research activities, but this is different from the R&D and spillovers discussed in the knowledge spillover theory because it is specifically internal. Again, universities (21.6 percent) and other commercial labs (8 percent) are ranked low, and are substantially smaller than the highest factors.

Next, we shift our questioning to the actual interaction with specific universities: Since its formation, which of the following types of relationships has your firm had with the following universities? UMKC, KU, and KU Med are the most relevant local universities, but we also extend the scope to Kansas State University, 120 miles west, and the University of MissouriColumbia, 126 miles east.

Table 4.4   Where do your new ideas come from?

Sources	%	Response
Mentors who give advice	52.5%	85
Customers and users	43.8%	71
Informal networks with other friends	42.0%	68
Internal R&D units	33.3%	54
Consultants	31.5%	51
Other firms in your industry	25.9%	42
Universities or higher education institutions	21.6%	35
Suppliers (materials, services, equip., etc.)	17.9%	29
Manufacturers	8.6%	14
Commercial labs or private R&D institutes	8.0%	13

Note: N=162.

While there is an apparent difference between UMKC, the most local institution, and the rest of the universities, the most common factor for all universities is "Hiring graduates" (from 15.6 percent to 23.7 percent). KU Med is a specialized institution, so it understandably has a completely different pattern here, and few firms have hired from KU Med. This hiring factor is intuitive because each university produces thousands of graduates every year, and hiring one graduate is not exactly the same factor of importance as other factors in this survey question, such as receiving training programs from a university. However, we should note its magnitude.

Focusing on UMKC, Kansas City's high-tech companies have had several forms of interactions: used business development services from the university (23.2 percent), taken courses (13.7 percent), taken training programs (10.9 percent), and used university staff as consultants (10.4 percent). While we cannot tell the content of the consulting services by the university, we find other teaching and training interactions present between local firms and universities. Some firms report being part of research consortia involving the university, so some form of research activity is present, while the ratio (6.2 percent) is substantially smaller than the other factors mentioned above. Additionally, the involvement by faculty is very low: only 4.3 percent for working part-time at the company or 1.9 percent for being part of a company's board. Reported equally low is licensing or patenting of research from a university (2.8 percent). These findings further

Table 4.5   Use of local university

	UMKC	U of Kansas	Kansas State	U of Missouri	KU Med
Using business development services offered by univ	23.2%	3.3%	0.5%	1.4%	1.4%
Hiring graduates	20.9%	23.7%	19.0%	15.6%	2.8%
Taking courses	13.7%	5.7%	3.3%	2.4%	0.0%
Training programs run by univ	10.9%	3.8%	0.9%	1.4%	0.0%
Univ staff acting as consultants	10.4%	2.8%	0.9%	0.9%	3.3%
Company staff teaching classes at univ	8.1%	10.4%	2.8%	2.8%	0.9%
Being part of a research consortium with univ	6.2%	5.2%	3.8%	1.9%	1.4%
Donations to univ	4.7%	7.1%	3.3%	3.3%	0.9%
Faculty members working part-time in your company	4.3%	2.8%	0.0%	1.4%	0.9%
Licensing or patenting of research	2.8%	3.8%	0.9%	0.5%	1.9%
Faculty on the company's board	1.9%	4.3%	0.5%	0.5%	1.9%

Note: N=211.

indicate that the business development or consulting services were not related to research or provided by faculty.

It is important to highlight that we designed the survey carefully and asked somewhat similar questions in order to minimize discrepancies from misconception or miswording, yet the results were highly consistent for all the questions, indicating that our survey questions were effective. Answers regarding regional advantages or disadvantages, sources of new ideas, and specific interaction with universities all led to the same picture: The talent is important, but the linkage to local research universities or other research institutions is a low-ranked factor. Within talent, firms report the importance of innovative people and technology, managerial, or marketing talent, and they report that mentors and customers are important sources of new ideas, but they tend to disassociate the talent of research from firm growth.

These findings are not constrained to the Kansas City area but are prevalent in other regions as well. Applying the concept of the Second-Tier Cities (Markusen et al. 1999), Mayer (2011), and Motoyama and Mayer (2017) used essentially the same survey questions to high-tech firms in three other cities: Seattle, Washington;

Portland, Oregon; and Boise, Idaho. Similar to Kansas City, these three regions host a good number of highly reputable high-tech companies; for instance, Amazon and Microsoft in Seattle, Intel in Portland, and Hewlett-Packard and Micron in Boise. Each area additionally hosts at least one research-intensive university. Particularly, the University of Washington in Seattle is the sixth largest in research expenditure among all universities, with $796 million in research spending. Boise State University is an exception as its classification is Large Master's University, but it has added doctoral programs in STEM disciplines since the 1990s.

The results are unequivocally similar. The access to innovative people and ideas is the most important factor for firm growth, followed by quality of life for staff and management and availability of managerial staff. The linkage to research universities or other research-oriented firms and the quality of research staff are the lowest factors for firm growth. Thus, our findings from the survey are not particular to Kansas City, but are present in other regions, and match with our nationwide regression results.

Table 4.6   Regional advantages in three other cities

Advantage Factors	Seattle	Portland	Boise
Informal local access to innovative people, ideas	4.31	4.23	4.16
Attractive local quality of life for staff and management	4.27	4.39	4.28
Local availability of managerial/professional staff	3.75	3.88	3.57
Access to local business services	3.16	3.35	3.49
Proximity to local customers	3.18	3.00	3.21
Access to local sources of capital, finance	3.14	2.83	3.12
Supportive local training organizations	2.25	2.70	3.04
Local shareholders	2.72	2.84	2.78
Proximity to local suppliers, subcontractors	2.94	2.98	3.09
Research links with other firms or organizations	2.57	2.72	2.70
Quality of local research staff	2.91	3.13	3.04
Research links with universities	2.13	2.65	2.69
Valid N	279	204	139

Source: Mayer (2011) and Motoyama and Mayer (2017).

4.3   INTERVIEWS OF 1 MILLION CUPS ENTREPRENEURS[3]

At 9:00 am every Wednesday, one entrepreneur comes up to a stage inside the Kauffman Foundation Conference Center. He or she presents a business idea for six minutes, which is not long enough to cover all the details, so it is a very high-level summary of how the company started, what the product or service is, and what kind of challenges the company is facing. The next 24 minutes are a Q&A session with the audience asking questions or making suggestions – usually in a friendly way, but occasionally in a challenging way. The presenter admits the flaw, defends the original idea, or thanks the audience and takes the suggestion. This is not a pitch to investors, like the TV show *Shark Tank*. In fact, nobody makes the decision of "thumbs up or down" at the end. This is not for judgment. Another entrepreneur takes the stage at 9:30 am, and this second round goes until 10:00 am.

This is an event called the 1 Million Cups (1MC) in Kansas City initiated by the Ewing Marion Kauffman Foundation in April 2012. It began as a small attempt by three foundation associates to engage with local entrepreneurs and community in Kansas City, and started with a modest audience of 13 people. However, something sparked. Every month, attendance doubled or even tripled. The September 2012 event had an audience of more than 100 people; the January 2013 event had more than 200. The energy of 1MC continued even after 10:00 am as hundreds of attendees stayed and networked at the conference center. Soon, entrepreneurs in other locations found 1MC attractive and wanted to replicate it in their cities. With no financial support from the Kauffman Foundation, volunteers in Des Moines, Iowa; St. Louis, Missouri; Houston, Texas; and Reno, Nevada started their 1MC programs in late 2012 to early 2013. By the end of 2016, 1MC had spread to 87 cities across the nation.

The Kauffman Foundation published two reports about 1MC based on two surveys (Konczal and Motoyama 2013; Motoyama et al. 2014). These reports documented that 1MC served as a place where entrepreneurs and "wannabe" entrepreneurs mingled. This pattern of mingling was confirmed in various ways to measure

---

[3]   This section was written with Arnobio Morelix and Colin Tomkins-Bergh.

entrepreneurs who were already working on a company (100 percent committed or having another job), generating revenue, and employing people. The self-identification of the attendees was mixed, ranging from entrepreneurs or managers, to engineer/developers, marketing professionals, and designers/creatives, while it tended to be heavily Caucasian (96 percent) and male (84 percent). Interestingly, although the majority of attendees were in the IT sector and tech-savvy with Twitter and other social media handles, the leading means of hearing about and deciding to attend 1MC was word of mouth (67 percent). Furthermore, there was no single dominant person spreading the word, but rather it was widely spread among various Kauffman associates and past 1MC attendees, a classic case of the snowballing effect and network expansion (Konczal and Motoyama 2013).

In this section, we analyze why people attended 1MC and what they perceived to have gained from it. This analysis not only demonstrates peer learning and its content between entrepreneurs, but also reveals the process of entrepreneurial development in the startup stage of companies and the use and integration of local entrepreneurship resources by entrepreneurs. To obtain such qualitative information, we targeted entrepreneurs who have presented at 1MC and conducted two focus groups and five individual interviews, totaling 16 entrepreneurs. We further supplemented with site observation at a number of 1MC events. In order to gain information about the development experience after 1MC, we further stratified by how long ago each person presented at 1MC: 0–2 months, 3–7 months, or 15–19 months.

The Value of Peer-To-Peer Learning

Why do they want to present their businesses at 1MC? Entrepreneurs are proud of their businesses and naturally want to talk about them. However, we found clearly that the motivation to present was not to promote the company, find new customers, or find investors, but to get connected and more specifically to receive feedback from other attendees. To structure the 24 minutes of interaction time, the 1MC organizers set up a panel of experienced entrepreneurs, usually at least two people, who kicked off by asking questions about marketing, pricing, management, and other aspects of running companies. Entrepreneurs reported a great deal of learning during their 1MC presentations when they were asked questions by the panelists and the audience. The panel and audience members offered constructive criticism and challenged presenters' assumptions, a crucial dimension of improving business ideas and operations. One participant emphasized the value of this critical process: "One good thing about 1 Million Cups is [the panelists] are not shy about telling you what they don't like. So we've received some areas to improve" (Entrepreneur A). The panelists' validation of assumptions was also helpful for entrepreneurs. A respondent noted, "I think . . . the dialogue we had [with panelists] validated assumptions about our business" (Entrepreneur B). These experiences, entrepreneurs emphasized, helped them refine their business models and build confidence in their businesses and in themselves. Conversations with audience members about presentations often spilled outside the 1MC meeting space.

Audience members with expertise in an entrepreneur's field could be particularly useful. One participant whose company made hot sauce explained he learned the most from someone with industry experience (note the famous Kansas City barbecue in the area): "One of the highest value things that came out of it is contact with someone who used to be in the barbecue sauce world. They had a connection with the hot sauce world and were able to make a list of the national hot sauce conventions" (Entrepreneur C).

Entrepreneurs noted that this interaction and learning had a lasting effect long after the presentation at 1MC as their businesses developed. The presenters found having a network of skilled entrepreneurs whose expertise and experiences were a phone call away was invaluable. One participant explained:

> A lot of it is having a network of people who can help you at different life stages. Can you tap into a network that says, "These are the kinds of things you need to think about [at this stage of business]?" Because what you did sixteen months ago, the skills you needed then are not the skills you need now. And the skills you need in sixteen months are not going to be the same skills you need in three years. (Entrepreneur D)

Another participant reiterated this idea: "I think what has definitely panned out [from 1MC] is people who are available to connect on a moment's notice and ask, 'I'm thinking about this compensation structure for these types of people. You have been through this, right?'" (Entrepreneur E).

Facilitating Local Connections

The presenters reported the growth of their local networks as a result of their presentation at 1MC, as well as the strengths of networks within the communities. The most common pattern was the creation of the second-degree connections, that is, new connections that were referred through other 1MC attendees who were not present at 1MC. As mentioned, 1MC organizers made it explicitly clear that the 1MC presentation was not for investors. However, the presenters reported getting connected with a wide range of supporters and collaborators in secondary and often unanticipated ways, such as customers, mentors, vendors, marketing firms, interns, even future local investors and donors.

These second-degree connections sometimes occurred well after the entrepreneurs' presentations at 1MC. One presenter described receiving an e-mail one month after his 1MC presentation from someone who was impressed with his work. This individual put him in touch with someone on a local steering committee for a major corporation. After several meetings, his company received a $225,000 investment from the corporation that allowed him to take his company in a new direction (Entrepreneur F). Similarly, another participant described how an attendee connected him to an important vendor:

> I also had a marketing and development firm reach out to me afterwards. She was at my presentation and afterwards looked at our website and realized we weren't functioning. She said, "I can help you find developers as well since you need that." It was such a great return considering what we thought we were going to get out of it. (Entrepreneur G)

Another presenter explained: "I now have a mentor because [this entrepreneur] actually reached out to me afterwards, and said, 'Hey, I'm interested and I want to help.' So he's dealt with me a couple times since our presentation and given me all kinds of feedback" (Entrepreneur H).

The second-degree connections included exposure to other local entrepreneurship events, programs, and classes. Based on requests from attendees, the 1MC organizers started to add a short announcement time at 9:30 am between the two presentations. This raised awareness and collaboration at the local level which the 1MC presenters also appreciated: "Sometimes the announcement in the middle of the presentation is the highest value of the day because it exposes you to things that are not on the radar" (Entrepreneur I).

1MC presenters, for instance, reported their engagement with the following local events and organizations: KCSource Link, Digital Sandbox, Sprint Accelerator, LEARN (a women's business education program), KC Chamber After Hours, Global Entrepreneurship Week, Urban Core, Mayor's Challenge cabinet steering community, Startup of the Year Brand Competition, and the KC Roundtable.

Ecosystem Catalysis

As we found in the previous section about the high-tech company survey, we anticipate mentors and informal networks could serve as important sources of new ideas. However, an important question for entrepreneurs is how to establish those connections specifically for their companies. Those informal networks, or even mentors, are not just "out there." In fact, one entrepreneur said she did not have any meaningful connections before attending 1MC. Starting to get connected by oneself without facilitation by specific organizations, programs, or events can be very difficult: "It sounds very small, but it's not, because it's hard to develop that network" (Entrepreneur F). Presenting at 1MC further helped to establish those connections.

In addition to the connections established between the presenters and the audience, countless new relationships were formed at each event among members of the audience. Hundreds of entrepreneurs, freelancers, service providers, and people from local corporations interacted and established relationships at each 1MC gathering, which ensured attendees became part of the local entrepreneurship community. 1MC's regular meeting time – every Wednesday from 9:00–10:00 am – created a go-to place for entrepreneurs and even those who were considering startups but were not connected to the entrepreneurial events. As 1MC became better known, it served as an entry point into the cities' entrepreneurial communities: "1 Million Cups was and is arguably still the cornerstone event of the Kansas City entrepreneurial community . . . We still tell everyone to go to 1 Million Cups. It was predictable; every week, when, and where" (Entrepreneur J).

Another entrepreneur noted that starting and running a company was such hard work that it trapped his working style into not getting connected outside. However, a weekly event like 1MC broke his cycle: "It changed our old-fashioned way. Every day, we would go to work. We would talk with customers, go home, and keep the books. Now with 1 Million Cups, it's a 180-degree change. We also do things for the others, because it has worked for me" (Entrepreneur K).

4.4 CHAPTER SUMMARY

The two sections of this chapter employ two different methods, a large-scale survey, as well as focus-group and individual interviews, but they complete one compatible picture. Moreover, that picture complements the findings from the nationwide quantitative analysis in Chapter 3.

The survey demonstrated that the companies in the high-tech sectors valued informal local access to innovative people or ideas, but, at the same time, the research-related factors came at the bottom of their list, such as research links with a local university or other firms, or the quality of research staff. Thus, the responding firms considered that the innovativeness was critical, but innovative people or ideas to be not related to research. This finding was consistent even if we asked similar questions phrased in different ways about regional advantages, regional disadvantages, and sources of their own firm development. Having said that, the high-tech firms had some level of interactions with local research universities in the forms of using business development services offered by universities or hiring graduates. Few companies noted using patents or licensing from universities, or having university faculty on the company's board.

The analysis of 1MC presenters revealed that entrepreneurs valued the peer-based learning from presenting their business ideas and receiving feedback. Such feedback and learning was not a one-time experience, but an ongoing process over a matter of months, or even a couple of years, that further developed as their businesses evolved to different stages and their people-based networks expanded through second-degree connections. The connections cultivated included a wide range of types, from customers, collaborators, and interns, to mentors and even investors.

At the same time, entrepreneurs reported that, despite the importance, it was not easy to establish a feedback system and networks of connections before attending 1MC. The difficulty of getting connected was observed even when a good number of entrepreneurship support organizations existed in the local area, meaning that a presence of people and organizations in an area does not warranty connections and learning between entrepreneurs. However, regular and visible events like 1MC initiated a go-to place for entrepreneurs, and the local ecosystem of entrepreneurship started to be better informed and co-ordinated.

In Chapter 5, we review another regional case study in St. Louis, which has gone through a major transformation of its entrepreneurship ecosystem in the last ten years. While this chapter about Kansas City primarily examined the high-tech sectors or entrepreneurs in the IT sector, as the past theory suggested a strong linkage between research activities and high-tech companies, Chapter 5 further investigates the general environment for both startup and successfully growing companies. We additionally examine companies in broader sectors, not constrained specifically to high-tech sectors.

5. How did the Gateway City transform its entrepreneurship? A case study of St. Louis

5.1 INTRODUCTION AND BACKGROUND

Commonly known as the Gateway City, St. Louis was a major regional center among Mississippian Native Americans before the European settlement (King 2002). The city was founded in 1764 by French fur traders and named after Louis IX of France, so-called the Sun King. It grew rapidly in the late nineteenth century and became the fourth-largest US city by the turn of the twentieth century after New York, Philadelphia, and Chicago (Arenson 2011). Brewing, bricks, shoes, milling, and paints were the major industries. In addition, the city's location along with the Mississippi River made it the national hub for transportation. While Chicago was generally known as the city with the most railway traffic (Cronon 1991), St. Louis was connected to the most cities by rail (Primm 1998).

St. Louis is known for the Gateway Arch, a 630-foot monument designed by Finnish-American architect Eero Saarinen in the 1960s. Ironically, people in Kansas City, contrasted in Chapter 4, considered the title of "Gateway to the West" stolen by St. Louis because Lewis and Clark departed from Kaw Point (now Kansas City), Kansas, in 1804 (Wyandotte County 2016). Calvin Trillin, a Kansas City poet, wrote of this sentiment satirically: "Yes, it is true that he [T.S. Eliot] was from St. Louis, which started calling itself the Gateway to the West after Eero Saarinen's Gateway Arch was erected, and I'm from Kansas City, where people think of St. Louis not as the Gateway to the West but as the Exit from the East" (Trillin 2011, page unknown).

However, the establishment of the Gateway Arch symbolized the declining legacy of the city itself. From its peak population in 1950, St. Louis started to experience stagnation in the following decades. Furthermore, within the region, population shifted westward from downtown to the suburbs. By the 1980s, the central city suffered from urban decay, rampant crime, and racial and economic divides. Throughout the 1990s and 2000s, St. Louis was listed as one of the FBI's most violent cities (FBI 2013). This was the pattern regularly observed in so-called former industrial rust belt areas, such as Detroit and Cleveland. Thus, this case of St. Louis may have many implications to other rust belt cities. As a reference, Ferguson, Missouri, the center of riots in 2014, was located in an inner-ring suburb northwest of downtown, at the edge of urban decay and adjacent to wealthy suburbs.

In addition to its declining manufacturing sectors, St. Louis has been largely known as a "big business" city and hosted many national and global companies during the last half century. It still is a major headquarters hub of logistics companies, such as United Van Lines and Mayflower Transit. Other large Fortune-ranked companies include: Energizer (batteries), Nestlé Purina Petcare (consumer food products), Express Scripts (pharmaceutical benefits management), Enterprise Rent-A-Car, and Emerson Electric, to name a few. However, the 1990s marked a further decline of the economy as several anchor companies were acquired and downsized. For example, Southern Bell Communications (now AT&T) relocated its headquarters to San Antonio, Texas, in 1993 (Pederson 2000); McDonnell Douglas was acquired by Boeing in 1996 (Knowlton 1996); Anheuser-Busch by Belgian-Brazilian company InBev in 2008 (De la Merced 2008); and mostly recently, Monsanto by German company Bayer in 2016.

With this image as a "big business" city, a director of entrepreneurship support organization expressed the landscape of regional entrepreneurship in this analogy:

> The typical problem I saw with entrepreneurs in St. Louis five years ago was like this: "I do this business alone, and I don't know other startups in town. I don't know investors here, and there is only old money by big corporations in St. Louis, so I go to Silicon Valley to find an investor." Then, if you talk to investors, they would say: "I don't find any prospective startups in St. Louis, and, in fact, there may not be any startups here, so I go to Silicon Valley to find companies to invest." So somehow, they might find each other in Silicon Valley, but not in St. Louis. (Brasunas, interview, December 10, 2012)

Since the prospects for job creation and economic recovery of the region by anchor companies seemed dim, this situation led to a series of reinventing reforms in the region by the public and private sectors, such as the state economic development agency, the Greater St. Louis Chamber, local universities, and prominent civic figures including John McDonnell and Bill Danforth (Motoyama and Knowlton 2016).

Two reinvention strategies emerged around 2010: the Mosaic Project to attract immigrants and the Arch Grants to promote entrepreneurship. We will examine the Arch Grants with details in the next section. However, up until the end of the 2000s, efforts to promote entrepreneurship were sporadic and unco-ordinated at the regional level. Some of the efforts and programs included: the CORTEX district as an innovation district; BioSTL (formerly the Coalition for Plant and Life Sciences) to promote the infrastructure for biosciences entrepreneurship; and Innovate VMS (Venture Mentoring Services, modeled after MIT) at Washington University in St. Louis (hereafter WashU). Nonetheless, each was an independent effort located in different parts of the city. CORTEX was between downtown and (east side of) WashU, and BioSTL was west of WashU near Clayton. More co-ordinated efforts started around 2000 with the establishment of T-Rex (short for Technology Entrepreneur Center at the Railway Exchange) in downtown St. Louis by the St. Louis Regional Chamber, Downtown St. Louis, and the City of St. Louis. T-Rex functioned as an incubator for startup companies and a hub of funding organizations, such as ITEN (technology entrepreneur support), Cultivation Capital (a venture capital), Capital Innovator (an accelerator), SixThirty (an accelerator), and Prosper (women entrepreneur support). The list in Table 5.1 shows the rapid expansion of entrepreneurship support organizations since 2010.

It has been remarkable to observe the emergence of an entrepreneurship community in recent years. In addition, the Business Dynamics Statistics revealed a sharp rise of startup activities in the region since 2010 (Census Bureau 2016). Our ground-level observations match with this statistical pattern as local stakeholders noted the substantial change in the landscape of entrepreneurship in the previous few years (Duttia, interview, August 24, 2012; Harrington, interview, December 10, 2012). Therefore, we investigate the case of St. Louis as a region transforming the fundamentals of its entrepreneurship ecosystem in a relatively short time with many implications to other rust belt cities.

Table 5.1   List of major support organizations in St. Louis

Organization	Founded	Target Group	Type
Missouri Venture Forum	1985	All	Networking, pitch
SLU Entrepreneurship Center	1987	All	Student support
Missouri Technology Corporation	1994	Tech, bioscience	Funding, programming
Regional Growth Capital	1994	All	Venture capital
Center for Emerging Technologies	1998	Bioscience, tech	Space, funding
Skandalaris Center (WashU)	2001	All	Student support
CORTEX	2002	Biotech	Office space
BioGenerator, BioSTL	2003	Biotech	Funding, lab space
Arch Angels	2005	All	Angel investment
Billiken Angels	2007	All	Angel investment
Gateway VMS	2007	All	Mentorship
ITEN	2008	Tech	Mentorship, programming
UMSL Entrepreneurship Center	2008	All	Student support
Arch Reactor	2009	All/products	Maker space
Nebula	2010	All	Incubator
The Mission Center	2010	Social	Incubator
Capital Innovators	2011	Tech	Accelerator
T-Rex	2011	Tech	Incubator
Accelerate STL	2012	All	Resource center
Arch Grants	2012	All	Grant
Cultivation Capital	2012	Tech, life science	Venture capital
Hive 44	2012	All	Incubator
Lab 1500	2012	All	Incubator
STL Venture Works	2012	All	Incubator
WEST	2012	Women	Mentorship
1 Million Cups	2013	All	Presentation forum
iSelect Fund	2013	All	Venture capital
SixThirty	2013	Fin-Tech	Accelerator
Cambridge Innovation Center	2014	All	Incubator
CLAIM	2014	All	Co-working space
St. Louis Makes	2014	Manufacturing	Research and events
Tech Artista	2014	All	Incubator
Prosper	2014	Women	Mastermind
Venture Café	2014	All	Networking, events
The Yield Lab	2014	Ag-Tech	Accelerator

Source: Motoyama and Knowlton (2016).

5.2 THE ARCH GRANTS AND STARTUP ECOSYSTEM[1]

As one of the regional reinventing efforts to establish economic drivers other than big businesses, four prominent local leaders established the Arch Grants program in 2012: Joe Schlafly, a venture capitalist and proponent of St. Louis economic development; Jerry Schlichter, a lawyer invested in the success of the region; Bob Guller, owner of a real estate management and investment firm; and Zack Boyers, a CEO with a background in banking. The goal of Arch Grants was "to advance economic development in St. Louis by attracting and retaining innovative entrepreneurs" (Arch Grants 2015). Arch Grants annually provided $50,000 equity-free cash for 15 to 20 startup companies based on its business plan competition. They targeted early-stage companies with unique and scalable ideas, and companies in any sectors could apply. In return, the recipient companies needed to locate their businesses in St. Louis for the following two years. It is worth noting that this kind of "small but many" venture funding marked a sharp contrast to the conventional venture funding by the public sector in which one or two winners get a large "lion's share," such as $1 million (Buffalo Billion 2016).

In addition to the financial support, Arch Grants provided other support, including pro-bono legal, accounting, and marketing services, introductions to local business and civic leaders, and relocation assistance (Arch Grants 2015). The primary purpose of this section is not to evaluate the effectiveness of those support services per se, but to analyze the behavior and development process of the recipient companies after the award. In other words, we will examine how those recipient companies progressed their businesses, what challenges they faced, and how they tried to overcome the challenges. Such analysis will deepen our understanding about the fundamental developmental paths of entrepreneurship and required resources, as well as the local system perspective.

Here, we conducted qualitative analysis through semi-structured interviews because we could analyze the rich context of business development and the recipient companies' other behavioral patterns. The structure of the Arch Grants offered the advantage of

---

[1]   This section was written with Karren Knowlton.

a manageable subject pool with wide coverage for this qualitative research. We asked the recipient companies about the nature of their businesses: how they started, what kind of challenges they faced, and what kind of resources they had used. Through that context, we analyzed the resource connection and networking patterns of the recipient companies; however, we were careful not to lead or assume with whom they networked or what kind of support they received. Like our interviews of the *Inc.* companies in Chapter 4, we did not ask whether they had worked with universities, but started to ask who helped them. Of 55 recipient companies during three cohort years from 201214, we were able to interview 46 of them. Based on the resources used by the recipient companies, we identified and interviewed 15 additional local support organizations, if the organization was mentioned at least twice by recipient companies.

Overall, we found that through participation in Arch Grants, individual firms experienced major evolution of their businesses, networks, and future opportunities; that is, many recipient companies reported the course of their businesses changed over time even though these were the winners of the business plan competition. Moreover, the evolution of their businesses came out of the feedback and interaction they received primarily from the other recipient companies, of the same cohort and previous cohorts. In addition, Arch Grants connected the recipient companies to key individuals and resources in the community which further helped the development of the businesses. At a higher level, Arch Grants served as a locus of connectivity for the larger entrepreneurial community by fostering an environment for collaboration and validation among support organizations in the region.

Importance of Peer-based Learning

More than two-thirds of the Arch Grant recipients expressed some form of meaningful interaction with other recipient companies. We consider "meaningful" interactions to be those that influenced the entrepreneurs or their companies and were more significant than simply knowing or seeing each other. For example, one company founder expressed it this way: "It's a great environment. I had some questions about some of the frameworks that they [another recipient company] are using, and sometimes other people stop by and ask me things: what do you think about this idea?" (IT Firm A).

The content of those interactions and learning varied, but we identified two categories. First, the recipient entrepreneurs went through the process of learning how to be an entrepreneur; that is, the entrepreneurs reported sharing knowledge of how to reformulate the business idea, how to interact with pro-bono lawyers, what type of funding might suit their company, how to select first employees, where to find them, or how to fire them. In essence, this was all about how to run a startup company.

This illustrates that writing a business plan or even winning the business plan competition was only one of the first steps for entrepreneurship, and entrepreneurs had to additionally learn the whole stack of knowledge necessary to start the companies and make them work. In other words, they had to learn a number of new processes and skills they were not exposed to at the business plan formulation stage.

Second, in terms of skills, the interaction between entrepreneurs developed to the expert acquisition stage, that is, passing on useful information specific to the other entrepreneur and function, such as coding in specific software or suggesting a change to a product concept or design.

> So, this guy came [in] yesterday, and he almost pulled my ears. He said "You're going to need more customers. You have enough traffic, and people that are engaged with you. Now you should put time in selling this." I said "OK, let's have a second conversation and see what you're doing on your side because you need more traffic." (IT Firm B)

Psychological Support among the Peers

Through the process learning and expert acquisition, the peer-based interaction also provided psychological support among the recipients; that is, it formed a community among the entrepreneurs through the common tie of closely observing each other and sharing exciting yet uncertain feelings about the entrepreneurial process. One entrepreneur expressed this as follows: "He [another recipient] is a nice guy and he's really intelligent. He gives me a lot of advice, but I know I also bother him. But all of us grant recipients are friends, and it's like a fraternity or sorority" (Other Firm A).

The interaction was not just from a single entrepreneur to another, but developed in to a group-based one. One entrepreneur even organized an "underground group" by pulling multiple entrepreneurs together to help each other navigate investment challenges. "We help run the Arch Grants Mafia. So we set up a meeting every month and all of that. It's just kind of a meeting we all have to talk about investors and situations" (IT Firm C).

Interaction Beyond the Industrial Sector

While the selection of Arch Grants was industry-neutral, every annual cohort distribution ended up as roughly a half in IT, a quarter in bioscience, and another quarter in other industrial categories (Imster, interview, February 13, 2014; Burke, interview, November 24, 2014). We observed that some of the peer interactions were based on a specific industrial sector by exchanging specific challenges and information. For instance: "What we wanted to do as the Arch Grants recipients and being in [the] life science space is that we wanted to get together and start working on these [government] grants ourselves. So, I'll get feedback from them on my grant and give feedback to them" (Biotech Firm A). The government grant referenced here was the SBIR grant, which many life science companies would apply for.

At the same time, there was much nonsector-specific information they valued and exchanged among the recipients in different sectors. "You're doing completely different things. You're all building something and that involves the kind of the same thought process, I like to think. Different expertise, but definitely the same thought process" (Biotech Firm B). Alternatively, another entrepreneur found this inter-sector exchange overlapping with the rough, uncertain, and emotional support discussed earlier: "It's just nice to have a little bit of a support group. The people maybe aren't in your same field, but are going through a lot of the same challenges" (Biotech Firm C). Once again, these statements underscore that the entrepreneurs faced major challenges, relied on peer entrepreneurs to get hints for solutions, and dealt with uncertainties.

Proximity to Enhance the Interactions

These social interactions did not form just through winning the Arch Grants; the spatial proximity also played a crucial role in creating such bonds. Arch Grants highly encouraged its recipient companies to use subsidized office space at the T-Rex incubator in downtown St. Louis, where the majority of the recipient companies located.

T-Rex also housed the Arch Grants administration and other entrepreneurship support organizations, and provided space for startups in the technology sector, hosting more than 100 startups (Patty Hagan, interview, September 11, 2014 and October 1, 2014).

This co-location catalyzed the learning among the entrepreneurs, and two entrepreneurs expressed it simply: "I crossed the hall to talk to the guy from [another AG company]" (IT Firm C); "The neighboring office here is also from [AG] biotech company, so we have really a lot to talk about, you know?" (Biotech Firm C). Another entrepreneur described this proximity effect as a "domino effect": "I definitely think that it's like a domino effect. So Arch Grants brings people here. T-Rex is where everyone is hosted, so you kind of run into people all the time" (Biotech Firm D).

Figure 5.1 describes the location of Arch Grants recipients (circles) and support organizations (triangles). The majority of Arch Grants companies were located at T-Rex in downtown St. Louis, and so were several support organizations. There was another cluster of companies and support organizations west, in the CORTEX area. Directly west of CORTEX was Forest Park, and farther west around Clayton was where WashU was located. Other than the downtown and CORTEX areas, the recipient companies were individually spread across suburban areas.

Multiple Layers of Supports for a Single Entrepreneur

The supports for the Arch Grants recipients came not only from the peer entrepreneurs and the Arch Grants staff, but also from a variety of other entrepreneurship support organizations in the area. Arch Grants played a direct role by providing facilitated introductions to other organizations. Moreover, we found that the relational validity of receiving the Arch Grants indirectly aided the recipient companies to seek out, or be sought out by, other support organizations. One entrepreneur described these continuing and expanding support relationships:

> Now that we're in Arch Grants, Capital Innovators [an accelerator] wanted us to join their program this fall, which we did. And we just got some funding from the Missouri Technology Corporation, so that's exciting. ITEN [a support organization] knocked on our door and they wanted us to join them, too. So, now that we're in the system. (IT Firm D)

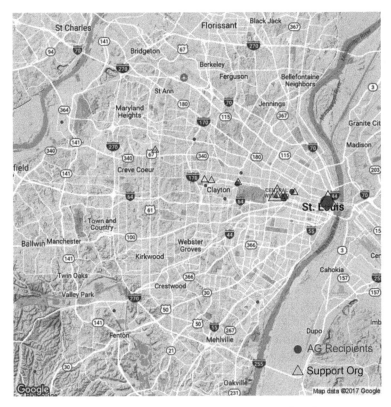

*Figure 5.1   Location of Arch Grants recipients and local support
organizations in St. Louis*

Similarly, these additional connections to other supports were not
limited to the first order, but had ripple effects. "Arch Grants got us
to ITEN, which got us to press, which put us in the business journal,
which put us in touch with some of our contracts. Further, ITEN
put us in touch with Capital Innovators, and they sent us a direct
invitation to apply" (Other Firm C).

Interviews further revealed mentoring relationships between
six recipient companies and four local individuals with previous
entrepreneurial experience. While we did not identify any specific
patterns of how the recipient entrepreneurs found those mentors,
the presence of these four mentors and their mentoring of multiple
Arch Grant recipients suggested that the way startup entrepreneurs

and experienced entrepreneurs met was not random: they met by attending one of the local entrepreneurial events, through a referral from unrelated acquaintances, or through an introduction from a support organization. Rather, the networks of those experienced entrepreneurs were within specific circles. Once startup entrepreneurs got into those circles, they were able to build mentoring relationships relatively quickly over the course of several months. These mentors were experienced business and civic leaders who were engaged in entrepreneurship and other local community activities.

Analyzing the supports and resources that Arch Grants entrepreneurs received, we further identified that the connections of the entrepreneurs expanded not only through support organizations and mentors, but also through local entrepreneurial events. Those events were organized by one of the support organizations, such as BioSTL, Lab 1500, and the Center for Emerging Technologies (mentioned in Table 5.1). Alternatively, we identified four other events that were operated not by formal organizations but by groups of grassroots volunteers, such as Start Louis, Build Guild, Code'Till Dawn, and Startup Weekend. These were monthly meet-ups among web professionals, solo entrepreneurs, and startup enthusiasts; all-night coding events; and group-based business plan exercises over a weekend, respectively.

In addition, two entrepreneurs mentioned the *St. Louis Business Journal* as giving valuable support, providing another kind of validity instrument by publishing an article about the company or giving an award such as "30 Under 30." This kind of media highlight opened up doors to valuable business connections, such as to new customers.

Thus, it is critical to conceptualize the support connections and local system of entrepreneurship beyond entrepreneurs and direct entrepreneurship support organizations to also include individuals, less formal events, and media. We mapped these network connections in Figure 5.2. For the visual simplicity of networks, we focused on connections mentioned by at least two firms in the 2013 cohort of Arch Grants recipients. The dark gray circles represent support organizations, such as Arch Grants at the center, mid-gray represents recipient companies, and white represents other miscellaneous individuals and events. The size of circle denotes the degree of connections. It became clear there were frequently used support organizations (dark gray) based on their locations near the center

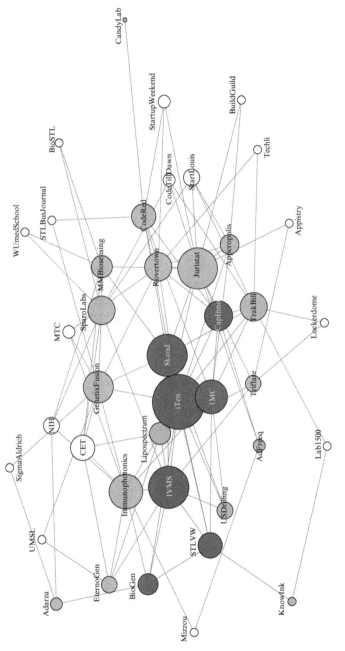

Figure 5.2   The network map of Arch Grants recipients and supports

and the large dot size – seven in total. Then, Arch Grant recipient companies (mid-gray) were surrounding those support organizations in the map. At the same time, there were 17 more miscellaneous individuals, events, and media (white) located outside of, yet providing different support functions for the startup companies. All these connections helped entrepreneurs grow their businesses.

Collaboration and Co-ordination between Support Organizations

It is equally important to highlight that multiple kinds of support each entrepreneur received came from the intentional collaboration and co-ordination between support organizations, that is, the connections between dark gray circles in Figure 5.2. While there was an availability of various resources by different support organizations, it was not a complete free-market system in which each entrepreneur atomically selected what he or she needed for the company, but rather the chain of resources became available through functional and strategic connections between support organizations. For example, three support organizations had a monthly brown-bag lunch for directors to exchange information: ITEN, a support organization for information technology companies; BioGenerator, a similar organization for biotech and pharmaceutical companies; and STL VentureWorks, an incubator space (Brasunas, interview, August 1, 2013; Gulve, interview, October 1, 2013; Sheridan, interview, December 9, 2013). The purposeful co-ordination was based on the crossover board memberships; for instance, among STL VentureWorks, Cultivation Capital, and ITEN. The executive director of Innovate VMS, a mentoring service, had her previous career at the Skandalaris Center at WashU. Thus, her tie to both organizations led them to a natural collaboration. Furthermore, two founders of Capital Innovators, an accelerator program, served as the mentors of companies supported by ITEN (Menietti, interview, November 15, 2013). Other less formal connections and co-ordination took place through jointly organizing events, attending events organized by other organizations, and serving on panels at those events.

For a startup company, receiving financial support through Arch Grants did not just advance their business: The timing was also crucial, and support from other organizations created a seamless bridging. One entrepreneur benefited from this collaboration among support organizations:

> At the demo day of the Capital Innovators, he [a private investor] approached us and said he's interested in investing. That helped us bridge between Capital Innovators and Arch Grants because we didn't get the money from Arch Grants until July 1. It also gave us a bargaining chip with Cultivation Capital [a venture capital]. (IT Firm E)

The same entrepreneur continued to describe other kinds of support he received: "Probably, our biggest mentor to date has been B.M., who was our lead advisor and mentor for Capital Innovators, and he's also a principal at Cultivation Capital. . ..We hired two students from WashU. The Skandalaris Center was already done matching students with companies" (IT Firm E). These statements demonstrated that the financial support from Arch Grants, an accelerator, and a venture capital did not materialize in isolation, but through strategic co-ordination between support organizations and the company.

Interviews further revealed that the directors of the support organizations exchanged highly detailed information about specific companies, such as what stage the company was in, what the strengths and weaknesses of the company were, and how they had worked with the company before (Harrington, interviews, December 10, 2012 and June 22, 2015; Brasunas, interviews, August 1, 2013 and February 13, 2014; Chmelir, interview, August 1, 2013). The periodic conversations between support organizations helped to avoid unnecessary and unintentional overlaps in support. Moreover, some support and training took place continuously through different support organizations and periods of time. The formulation and reformulation of a business plan and the expansion of one's customer base were not one-time events, but a continuous process over time helped by different support organizations (Motoyama and Knowlton 2016).

5.3   INTERVIEWS OF HIGH-GROWTH FIRMS IN KANSAS CITY AND ST. LOUIS[2]

We continue to examine the entrepreneurial process at the firm level through interviews of high-growth firms. Here we analyze

[2]   This section was written with Jim Brasunas, Francis Chmelir, Steve Johnson, Jordan Bell-Masterson, Brian Danley, and Arnobio Morelix.

Inc. companies, just like in our regression analysis, but deepen our analysis as interviews can provide much richer information about structural and developmental processes of firms. There are two advantages of using the *Inc.* list for interviewing companies. First, as mentioned in Chapter 3, the *Inc.* firms have at least $2 million in annual revenue; thus, they have accomplished a certain scale of their businesses and provide insights not only about how companies have started, but also about how companies have successfully survived and scaled up. Second, a nationally known magazine publisher constructs this list based on economic criteria, with the revenue scale and growth rate, so it is different from the conventional snowballing sampling method, in which you get referrals from your interviewees, and reduces the potential self-selected behaviors and network effects of those companies.

We have again targeted firms in the information technologies and life sciences sectors as these high-tech sectors are supposed to be technology- and innovation-intensive. Nationwide, IT firms constitute 19.4 percent, and life sciences firms 6.5 percent, of *Inc.* firms (Motoyama 2015). We further add firms in the business services sectors (10.2 percent) as we have observed the high use of IT and other forms of technologies in business services. Moreover, as we discuss in the analysis, many companies operated somewhere in the middle of the sectoral boundary between IT and business services.

We conducted these *Inc.* company interviews in both Kansas City and St. Louis with the same interview questions. In Kansas City, we identified 43 firms in these three sectors on the *Inc.* list between 2007 and 2011 and contacted all of them. Four companies declined our interviews, and we could not get any response or current contact information for 14 companies. One company moved out of the region, and we did not contact one company as we learned from other sources the founder was having health issues. This resulted in 23 interviews out of 43 companies, thus reaching more than half of the entire list (53 percent).

In St. Louis, there were 52 firms in these three sectors. We stratified and narrowed the list to 26 firms by randomly selecting within each of the three sectors. Of these firms we contacted, nine firms responded to interviews (34 percent).

In both cities, there is no statistical difference between interviewed firms and non-interviewed firms in terms of revenue, employees, and growth rate, except we were unable to interview the three largest firms

Table 5.2   Descriptive statistics of Inc. firms in the Kansas City region

	Interviewed Firms (23)			Non-Interviewed Firms (20)		
	Revenue	Employees	Growth rate	Revenue	Employees	Growth rate
Minimum	2,013,710	8	18.6%	2,537,000	10	16.8%
Maximum	336,500,000	650	3,389.0%	4,420,775,411	675	1,800.5%
Mean	34,747,987	131	440.7%	249,837,286	151	227.8%
Median	8,664,810	52	99.3%	13,823,182	93	97.4%

Table 5.3   Descriptive statistics of Inc. firms in the St. Louis region

	Interviewed Firms (9)			Non-Interviewed Firms (43)		
	Revenue	Employees	Growth rate	Revenue	Employees	Growth rate
Minimum	$2,100,000	14	72.0%	$2,000,000	2	5.4%
Maximum	$61,198,222	410	360.6%	$555,000,000	4900	816.1%
Mean	$15,613,216	90	149.5%	$46,709,302	251	154.9%
Median	$8,604,000	39	96.5%	$7,400,000	46	96.0%

in the two regions, which had revenues from $228 million to $4.4 billion. We consider that this omission of the very large firms does not undermine our analysis because the nature of business operation and sources of growth for those very large firms would be different. For instance, a revenue growth of $100 million may likely come from acquisition of other firms. What we analyze throughout this book is entrepreneurs, their firm development processes, and their connections to the local systems in the sense of Schumpeter's definition of innovations, that is, creating new products, new technologies, new organizations, and new markets which are internally generated at the firms, not externally acquired. Thus, overall, we consider our interviewed companies to demonstrate a fair representation of *Inc.* high-growth and innovative firms in the two regions.

While we found some differences between firms in Kansas City and St. Louis in specific sources of entrepreneurial support, which was anticipated, we came to highly compatible findings in the two regions regarding two questions in our interviews: *What is the nature of your business?* and *Where did your firm growth come from?*

The analysis of these two questions is important because they can uncover the fundamental entrepreneurial process in the startup and scale-up phases. Note that these are relatively open-ended questions, and interviewees could comment freely without being biased toward the role of technologies, patents, universities, or other factors that we have hypothesized and investigated so far.

Growth Based on Market Niche

The most fundamental finding here is the growth of those *Inc.* firms based on having a clear market niche of their own. Here, we mean the market niche as the explicit identification of market demand, as well as the positioning of the company's product or service within the market. Moreover, the market demand did not need to be large, such as revenue in billions or the global market, but the demand had to meet specific demand not met at all, or certainly not met better, by other competitors in the market.

For instance, IT Company A's business was in data and server maintenance service specifically in the Kansas City region. The two founders explained that the cost of inputs, such as space, electricity, and labor – the standard factors of consideration in economics – meant little for their business because what mattered most in their market was reliability and speed of recovery when their client's server went down. Regardless of their own service quality or that of any other competitor, it was a stylized fact that any server would go down once to a few times a year. The question was how quickly they could recover it so their client could go back to their normal business. Using the most highly trained engineer in Silicon Valley, or the cheap one on the Southeast coast, would not provide an advantage in this matter because it could take hours or even a day until an engineer could come to the site and start to analyze the problem. In contrast, this company could send an engineer within an hour to the client's site and bring back the system within a few hours at maximum. Interestingly, the two founders expressed that a local economic development agency was unsupportive of their business idea because it could not be scaled up to other regions. The founders said, "They didn't understand us, and we didn't need to scale up in other places. We said 'forget it' and went ahead with our business" (IT Company A).

Business Service Company J operated creatively between the education and IT sectors. Among educational institutions, superintendents at school districts or secretaries at states were the decision makers of which hardware or software programs to purchase. Traditionally, this field was dominated by publishers who sold textbooks, and superintendents were conservative, meaning that none of them wanted to be the first to implement a new technology or program until other districts had implemented it first. Another aspect of this market was that none of the superintendents were technologically proficient because they were teachers or managers of schools, and how well a company was known to superintendents was critical to making sales. The founder of this company had the right experience, connections, and reputation in the field because of his experience running the sales division at Apple and selling computers to districts and states. He played a broker role between superintendents and software companies by providing reliable information about technologies and distribution channels. For instance, publishers were national players and only interested in selling hardware and software products that would reach the national scale. Moreover, superintendents were oriented toward teacher-based solutions if students were struggling, but lacked information about what kind of technology-based education programs were available to reach those struggling students. This company was able to exercise knowledge of both the educational management and technology sides and could speak in professional yet approachable language.

IT Company B specialized in developing a system for legal services, primarily for legal departments of large corporations. Their business model was based on "the fact that the legal profession is a pretty backward profession in general IT" (IT Company B). Essentially, they built search technology, repository-type technology, and dashboarding and reporting tool technology to layer on top of more established types of legal platforms. They explained that their company's strength lay in its identification of markets that were underserved and its ability to run quickly. "Any time you start a business, you have to have something unique, something proprietary, whether it be a technology or even an approach to the market" (IT Company B).

Health Company A established a drug-testing device which was primarily used for employers to screen for recruitment. Their technology was unique because the device had to differentiate leisure-oriented drugs and painkillers, particularly opiate-based, as the latter could stay in the body a long time after someone had been hospitalized. (Otherwise, about a quarter of the US population would screen positive for these substances.) However, the company president emphasized that their strength was not just based on the technology or device, but also based on their large-scale information system. He explained that their clients were not hospitals, but large-box retailers, who would hire hundreds of thousands of employees per year. Thus, what's essential for the clients was hundreds of testing centers corresponding to their employment centers throughout the nation, and the whole system to conduct tests, manage the results, and maintain the database. "While everyone else viewed it as a medical service business, we viewed it as a medical and information service business" (Health Company A). The founding entrepreneur described how they situated the technology and core of their business: "I think the technical word for us is a technology-enabled service provider. In other words, we took a very boring, backwater industry that nobody wanted to be in and nobody could make money in, and we applied technology to it."

Business Service Company B operated between hospitals and patients. With rising costs of healthcare and insurance, many patients left the hospitals with bills but were unable to pay. This company not only tracked patients, but also arranged through Medicaid, the Social Security Administration, and indigent, crime victim, and other federal, state, and county programs that would cover any expenses for patients. Its revenue model, therefore, was obtaining a certain percentage reimbursement for hospitals and benefits for patients. The entrepreneur described it as a "low-technology, high-service business" for which he got the basic concept when he was running his previous cleaning business, also a low-tech, high-service company. He continued to describe the essence of his business model as "really about bringing people to the product to a problem and solving it."

Business Service Company C provided packaging and shipping materials to other companies. While that sounds ordinary, their niche was to deliver in smaller and more regular quantities so their clients did not have to keep large inventories. This distinction was important because packaging and shipping materials were bulky, and the standard distribution service through UPS or FedEx was not cost efficient. Consequently, the inventory would require a large space, and many companies had incentives to keep this cost low. The CEO described the landscape of the sector:

The national competitors sell their things and they've got a very large corporate mentality that doesn't always fit, so the customer gets kind of tied up in that and penalized. They gotta take the delivery when the delivery is going to be there. If they don't have a minimum order that satisfies those companies, they can't have it. So I think more than the just-in-time, but it's "we're glad to take your order any time at any level." Having the product on the floor is very important. Many of our competitors like to be more of a broker rather than a distributor. We like to be a distributor more than a broker. It's that simple, but honestly that's what I saw on the market, a void there.

The ways the growth companies established their own market niche were so unique that no single prescription could apply. After all, this is the core of what entrepreneurs do. The identified niche could be within a specific market, such as IT Company A's server maintenance focused in Kansas City and Business Service Company C's small-batch distribution of packaging materials. Alternatively, companies identified niches between markets, such as Business Service Company A between the IT and education markets, and Health Company A between IT and medical services.

In additional, it is worth noting that the market niche of each company did not correspond to businesses of local anchor companies such as Cerner, Sprint, DST, Garmin, or Hallmark in Kansas City. Of the identified 43 *Inc.* companies in the region, 22 of them were in business services and 15 were in IT. Thus, we initially hypothesized that each sectoral cluster was a representation of the local sectoral conditions. However, we found that none of the *Inc.* firms had those anchor companies as clients. Having said that, we did find that some of the *Inc.* firm entrepreneurs had early careers with local anchor companies, namely Cerner and Sprint. Each had gained valuable experience at the local anchor companies, but their prospective new businesses were neither related to the respective sectors, nor did they have the anchor companies as major clients.

The Need for Changes and Pivots

The second major finding from the interviews was that, while each company had a clear concept of its own market niche, its core business was not permanent, and the company had to keep making incremental changes or sometimes major changes – what the entrepreneurs called "pivots."

Business Service Company A specialized in the development and licensing of a data system for educational institutions. According to the *Inc.* list, Company B was categorized as a business service firm, but such a categorization was unimportant for the company, and their business area intersected with IT, business service, and education. The founder had successfully run and sold two businesses before, and decided to launch this company because he found a clear demand. Educational institutions needed an alumni database because alumni were the sources of money and the best examples of the success of the school. Furthermore, those institutions wanted to own and manage data in their own way because it was proprietary information, so a highly standardized data system was not desirable. Nonetheless, they did not have the expertise to create and manage such a data system on their own. Thus, the solution was this company's creation of the data system and licensing of it to client companies. The founder started the business working with a local high school.

The entrepreneur of this company described that the types of clients shifted quickly at the beginning of their business. They, in fact, started with a local education district, but soon realized that revenues from public schools or districts were not sufficiently profitable. Thus, they shifted to target local private schools. This shift was based on their observation that alumni from public high schools did not have much affiliation to their alma maters, but alumni from private high schools did, justifying the use of the database by their clients. Over time, this company expanded its database to colleges and even expanded its operation throughout the nation. It became one of the leading companies in this area, and its clients include the top tier private universities, such as MIT and Carnegie Mellon, and the largest public universities, such as Arizona State University. Moreover, this company made daily efforts to add and improve its system functions. Since a few major local universities were clients, they sent their development engineers to their clients for a couple of hours every month. "The best thing you can do is go to a local client. I don't care who you are [in rank or title]. Sit down and see how they use our technology. That's going to make us and you more successful. Or you will be left behind in the market quickly."

The CEO of Business Service Company D had his former career at the FBI and then worked at a startup company that ran background checks for insurance companies about theft and fraud issues. He joined this company to expand its background check business, which required assembling a variety of information from judicial and law enforcement documents. However, the documentation of judicial and law enforcement branches was not standardized or digitized, so one needed specialized knowledge of where, how, and what information to obtain, as well as knowledge of how to systematically organize it. The CEO started a background check business for employer recruitment, and that was their core business for the first ten years. Then, they identified that a similar background check business could apply to school admissions as medical, dental, and law schools were increasingly keen on knowing the past records of their prospective students. The fees from each individual background check for schools would be smaller compared to the more comprehensive background checks performed for corporate employment, but because the number of requested school background checks would come in bulk, it generated high revenue.

IT Company C provided network infrastructure for corporate clients including both hardware and software. The company had a strong clientele in the medical, legal, financial, and education sectors, and state and local governments; moreover, they focused on their "underserved markets" in the broader Midwest area, such as Denver, Kansas City, and Omaha. The national competitors in this business area, such as Dell, played dominant roles in major geographic areas, such as New York, Los Angeles, and Chicago. However, this company operated on the "high-touch" dimension of the network infrastructure business which companies could not scale up in different geographic areas. Thus, IT Company C was still competitive in the underserved markets where the scale economies of the nationwide competitors could not apply.

However, this company had to go through a major transition. The company started in 1992, and its network infrastructure was based on Novell. This selection was based on the then-standard practice that the CEO had experienced with IBM, his previous employer. Nonetheless, by the late 1990s, he realized that Novell was becoming less competitive and foresaw that the future of the industry would be based on the Microsoft-based network system. The CEO described it as literally a wake-up call for their business: "In 1996, I woke up about 4:30 am one morning and wrote a memo to other executives saying, 'we're moving from Novell to Microsoft, Novell's gonna die. If we don't switch before most people realize, we're gonna die.'"

The origin of Health Company B goes back to 1896 when the CEO's great-grandparents started a retail laundry business to wash personal clothing. In the 1950s, the CEO's father expanded with a new division of linen supply to hospitals. When the CEO and his siblings took over the business ten years ago, they initially focused on the linen supply business and sold other divisions. However, the CEO emphasized, "We're still a brick and mortar business. It's very capital and labor intensive, although we take advantage of this pretty significant amount of technology. Then, we need to be where the growth is going to be." They transformed during the last ten years by expanding their linen supply business into a medical supply business specifically targeting acute care hospitals, surgery offices, and private practices where the demand was relatively small and changed frequently. Essentially, they leveraged their supply chain function based on linens, but expanded to other medical procurement items. They have also expanded geographically to St. Louis and Denver.

The Presence of Business Mentors

The third finding from the interviews was the prevalence of support that these entrepreneurs have received over time. Most importantly, over three-quarters of entrepreneurs mentioned that they had some form of formal or informal mentors. For instance, the entrepreneur of Business Service Company C described:

> Mr. G. was a mentor for me early on. He was very willing to help on the legal side, putting the operating agreement together. Challenged me to think about. . . . He kept me between the ditches early on. I have to contribute a lot to Mr. G. as a mentor. He didn't give us revenue, but he gave me direction.

Business Service Company E operated wholesale distribution to education, hospitals, churches, and governments. The entrepreneur recalled his crisis in the late 2000s and the interaction between him and his mentor.

> I knew I was in trouble and I called [my mentor], B.H, but I didn't know how much trouble I was in. . . . So we sat in my mentor's office, and I told him what was going on. B. said "you're going to lose your shirt.". . . That [conversation] forced us to take a serious look at margins, profitability, marketing, and advertising. We had to really re-evaluate. . . . Later, I told

B. that we were going to start calling on corporations and hospitals [to expand our markets]. And he asked, "How good are you at the market you're in?" and I said "we're OK." Then he said, "Until you get really good, you don't go into another market."

Business Service Company F was established by three partners. They were previously in the human resources business and were frustrated by the industry practice in which the staffing agency tried to take a larger margin by charging its clients as much as possible, while paying the temporary staff as little as possible. "There's all this secrecy and shrouded stuff that nobody is allowed to talk about." Instead, when the three partners launched the company, their philosophy was to train the staff for skills to meet the market demand and pay both sides reasonably. They believed it would create a positive cycle of better staff staying with the company for a longer time, with higher satisfaction from the client companies, who were willing to pay the premium. Within the first ten years of operation, they have successfully expanded their areas of staffing from clerical to IT and medical services.

Two of the three partners had mentors for the company. One of the partners' fathers operated real estate businesses in multiple cities and provided part of the initial capital for this company. Then, he continued to be a "silent partner":

> Someone who can be a mentor when you need [one]. It's been an unbelievable situation for all three of us, that we have an open door to go to down the hall when we need advice, yet at the same time truly a "silent partner" who's not breathing down our necks and our business every day, but there for guidance, help, support, and certainly financial help.

Another partner joined the Helzberg Entrepreneurship Mentorship Program (HEMP) to seek a formal mentorship. HEMP was established by Barnett Helzberg who sold Helzberg Diamonds to Warren Buffet's Berkshire Hathaway in 1995. Helzberg was formally mentored by Ewing Kauffman, a well-known local entrepreneur who operated Marion Labs, a pharmaceutical company, and established the Ewing Marion Kauffman Foundation dedicated to the promotion of entrepreneurship and education. Helzberg was grateful for Kauffman's mentorship and asked one day: "Mr. K. [Kauffman's nickname], you have been so generous to me. What can I do for you?" Kauffman's answer was simple. "That's okay. You will help someone someday" (interview, December 18, 2012). Inspired by those words, Helzberg had mentored a good number of entrepreneurs from time to time, but upon his retirement in the late 1990s, he decided to establish a formal mentorship program by partnering with five other renowned local entrepreneurs, including Henry Bloch, co-founder of H&R Block, the nationwide tax filing company.

While HEMP started to take only three to four mentees per year, it had grown to accept 10–15 mentees every year and matched each with a mentor from their list of 75 fellows, local entrepreneur mentors that Helzberg had cultivated over the years or mentees who had gone through the program before (HEMP 2011). Their one-year, one-on-one mentorships took place about once a month, but varied by the agreement between the mentor and mentee. Since the mentorship required complete confidentiality, Helzberg and the program administrator were not aware of the discussed content. However, Helzberg noted that, in his experience, the topics could cover anything involving running companies, from a cash-generating model, market positioning, marketing, or ownership, to work–life balance.

A different chain of connections formed other lines of entrepreneurial mentorship in the region. The founding partner of IT Company A formerly worked at Arthur Andersen, the nationally operating consulting company, and was mentored by Neal Patterson, who later co-founded the Cerner Corporation, one of the local anchor companies in town. It turned out that Patterson had himself been mentored by Ewing Kauffman.

In one fortunate case, the founder of Business Service Company J had experience at Apple, as described before, and he considered Steve Jobs as his role model in the 1980s. This founder proudly displayed a frame containing Jobs' autograph and a little drawing of the first Macintosh computer.

> If you read anything on Jobs, all that is true. That is how it was. Nothing was impossible. No one said no to us. That did make an indelible impact on me. If you imagine, if you can think of it, just go do it! I learned a great deal about myself, building effective teams, nurturing, earning respect, and earning a market. (Business Service Company J)

Reflecting this series of mentorships and support relationships, the entrepreneurs of high-growth companies characterized the environment for entrepreneurship in Kansas City or St. Louis as highly positive. They often described each city as "a small town" (IT Company

D). They described the accessibility of people and support with "a small degree of separation" (IT Company C) or "six degrees of separation" (IT Company A). Alternatively, some described it as "a big town, but small enough to feel comfortable reaching out to new people with referrals and ask for help" (Business Service Company D).

In addition to mentors, the entrepreneurs pointed out other kinds of supporters who were happy to connect people with the right expertise.

> I also think there's just a body of individuals here, for example in the legal community, who were sort of connecters. They try to connect A to B and B to C. [G. K.] would be a good example of somebody who knows everybody. He is really steeped in the venture community here. (Health Company A)

The Locally Recruited and Trained Talent

The fourth finding is related to workforce, or "talent" in the entrepreneurs' language, more specifically the types of talent wanted and the availability in the region. While current convention emphasizes the STEM (Science, Technology, Engineering, and Math) workforce or IT and coding skills, high-growth companies did not express their talent search in that direction. Instead of those specific skills, the growth companies sought people with high aptitude. In a nutshell, such aptitude can be described as young, smart, and motivated people. "We don't go for senior programmers, but we recruit younger programmers who are smart and up-and-coming. If they're on a project at [a local major firm], they're probably on a very limited part of the project. Here, we give them exposure and let them do the whole thing" (Health Company A).

A CEO of a different company elaborated in this way:

> Number one, we look for someone who wants to make a difference at a smaller company. I can't think of a better term right now; kind of go-getters: [an] "I don't want to work for a big machine; I want to make the machine run myself" mentality. We look for people who are also really energetic, very cooperative in the assessments we do. We also look for people who don't require a lot of structure because we don't have time to micromanage anybody. Our clients demand how our daily schedules go. You can walk in today and say "I want to accomplish these ten things today" and not touch a one of them because of one phone call. If a client

calls and says "I've got an issue or I need help with X," your entire day can change. So we have people who are very flexible, very adaptable, and if they're expecting rigid structure, they're going to hyperventilate here. (Business Service Company D)

The growth companies in Kansas City and St. Louis highly rated the availability of talent with those kinds of high aptitude. Compatible with the quotes above, another company CEO described:

The reason why we're here is the availability of IT resources. Good, reasonably priced programmers are really the reason. We're picking people at a stage in their career where I think they're particularly productive, and I think they want an exposure to a broader variety of training and projects. If I try to compete with [a large local company] for their best programmers, it would never work. (IT Company B)

Health Company A has a branch in Richmond, Virginia, and the CEO described that they had to rely on the University of Virginia as their talent source, if they were lucky enough to get any. On the other hand, he described the talent availability in the Kansas City region as excellent and reliable.

We've done a lot of things here that couldn't be done other places. The quality of people we get here as far as employees . . . if there's someplace that has a better pool, I'm not sure where it is. Excellent education backbone here helps provide very good, ready-to-go employees.

It is important to note that what the companies considered as excellent talent came not only from local major research universities, such as the University of MissouriKansas City (UMKC), the University of MissouriColumbia (Mizzou), the University of Kansas, (KU), and Kansas State University (K-State), and Washington University in St. Louis, but also from other smaller public and private universities in the region. "All the institutions around here do a great job, whether it's trade schools, UMKC, Rockhurst, KU, Mizzou, K-State, William Jewell [College], or Park [University]. Smart people are not the issue" (IT Company E).

Thus, the commonly observed pattern was the recruitment of young, smart, and motivated talent who were often fresh or recent graduates of local universities. Moreover, this strategy was matched with their corporate training practices. Essentially, the high-growth companies trained these talented workers for one or two years to acquire specific technical skills needed for the company.

> For the things we do, you can get a lot of very good people who, in a short period of time, can come up to speed on the kinds of things we do. We put them through a pretty rigorous certification process with Oracle, get them trained up in a certain technology, shadow them in a couple of projects, and six months later they're billable. They're productive members of the team. (Business Services Company G)

Health Company C invested substantially in its IT system, and its founder illustrated that training up to a certain level was only one dimension of talented workforce management. Another dimension required methods and culture to keep them up to date with technology. "Our IT engineers want to go [to] the Microsoft EA [Enterprise Agreement] events and hear what's up-and-coming and play with the latest tools." He additionally emphasized that they had to let the engineers tap into the larger, global community of IT engineers so they kept learning and being inspired.

Related to talent, entrepreneurs often referred to the importance of the "Midwestern work ethic." Entrepreneurs elaborated that this meant employees with "great work ethic" were "loyal" (Business Services Company A), "polite," and "reasonable" (IT Company E). One interviewee summed it up in this way: "Kansas Citians are extremely hard-working and bust their ass" (Business Services Company H). Another CEO who used to live in Northern and Southern California said by contrast that "you had to give someone [in California] a BMW if they were going to come write code for you" (Health Company A).

Entrepreneurs commented that such a work ethic contributes to workforce retention:

> We have a really solid core group of employees with a lot of longevity right now, and you don't find that in our industry. It's really typical for people to spend six months, a year – I'm talking about internal employees. Contractors jump, and that's normal. But the core internal employees, we have people who have been with us six years, five years; even three years is a long time in this business. And we take care of them financially; they feel like part of our culture. We have a really unique culture here, which I think is part of it. (Business Services F)

Moreover, entrepreneurs saw that the work ethic and courtesy rooted in the regions led to the core strengths of their companies, particularly in service-oriented sectors:

> There is an advantage. We have a lot of clients all over the country, and we have a lot of clients on the coasts, but I do zero marketing/advertising

on either coast. I think a lot of people on the coasts like working with Midwesterners because we're nice. That may sound stupid, but we hear from clients all the time in New York, L.A., and San Francisco that we just do things differently here and we're nice. We're courteous. People aren't in a rush to get you off the phone. If you call in with a problem, people actually answer it. People will actually talk to you. (Business Services Company D)

Prevalence of Bootstrapping and Self-Finance

The last finding from the interviews was the patterns of finance among these high-growth companies. While the gold standard for entrepreneurship today is to write a business plan and get funding from VCs, we found few examples fitting this pattern. Instead, the entrepreneurs started small, captured specific clients quickly, and scaled up their businesses based on their own revenue. Here, we need to keep in mind that these *Inc.* firms have successfully scaled up to multiple millions of dollars in revenue.

The CEO of Business Services Company B described that his startup cost was only around $30,000 or $35,000, but he was able to grow the company quickly. "It's basically organic. We just continue to market and continue to grow." Another entrepreneur was still running his previous business, but was able to capture one of those clients as a new customer for his new business. He recalled the beginning of his new business with precise dates and funding:

> Fortunately, I had one of my big clients interested in funding this. From November 23 to April 29, they funded a pilot. We built out a product that was specific to them, and at the end of that they said yes. They signed up for an enterprise agreement that paid us $50,000 a month. We then built that entire platform. (IT Company D)

The choice of this bootstrapping finance method was not due to the lack of venture capital money in the region, but rather was strategic and intentional. One entrepreneur concisely summarized: "All growth is incremental, which is a beautiful thing" (Business Services H). Moreover, several entrepreneurs emphasized that it was important for them to control their financing because taking external private equity meant the loss of ownership of the company. "It's important to take control of our own. Our company came from really the core beliefs that we are going to grow the company [in] the traditional way: we are going to go out, get clients, create revenue and control our expenses, and have a profit" (IT Company A). "We never had to get a loan or venture, angel, [or] mezzanine financing at all. We paint the walls and keep the carpet clean, and that seems to work better for us. No debts, no loans. We're in great shape in terms of that!" (Business Services Company C).

In one case, the two co-founders said they discouraged the business model using VC finance when they delivered a lecture at their alma mater:

> Actually down at Mizzou [University of MissouriColumbia] last year, they had us teach this class on venture capital, and we said, "We've never used it; we don't see a need for it." [*laughs*] So no funding from that standpoint. Luckily, the margins were good enough to keep growing organically and run it as conservative as possible.

Of 32 interviewed companies, two had used equity finance from VCs. One company followed a similar self-finance and bootstrapping strategy, but accepted external capital in recent years not for the reason of scaling up. Here, the CEO first described the sequence of financing:

> I personally funded the company for the first six to nine months, and then we had about [a] $2 million angel round that came in at the very beginning. Then we raised about another $3–4 million in a second round with C. Capital. Then S. Capital came in and put in about $10 million or $11 million after that. (IT Company B)

However, his further explanation gave a nuanced understanding about the process of company growth and investment. To the question of how the company found the VC, he replied:

> They approached us. We probably get one or two inquiries every week by different investors that are looking to become part of our company or to invest money. And most of the time, we're not interested because we're not in the mode of raising money. In different cases, they are brands. VCs actually helped us gain credibility to recruit good talent, which helped us quite a bit as we evolved. (IT Company B)

This explanation provides an alternative view of the role of VCs. Conventionally, VCs are considered as the agents that fund business ideas and early stage companies to make growth happen. Indeed, the National Venture Capital Association claims that they "transform breakthrough ideas into emerging growth companies that drive U.S. job creation and economic growth" (NVCA 2016). However, this case suggests that venture capitals were seeking already-growing firms in which to make investments. The role of VCs, then, is to make the growth faster or possibly larger, but not necessarily as an agent to make the growth happen.

The common practice of bootstrapping does not necessarily mean entrepreneurs had no trouble in finance. Two interviewees mentioned a gap in funding of between $500,000 and $3 million, particularly because of the nature of software or medical services, for which they could not provide collateral to get loans from banks.

We had an opportunity to collaborate with *Inc.* magazine and distributed a survey at the national scale. We received 479 responses, and one of the questions asked about the financial source: What sources of financing have you drawn from to finance your current business? Please check all that apply.

This result was compatible with the interviews conducted in Kansas City and St. Louis. Entrepreneurs financed most commonly from personal savings, and also leveraged loans and credit cards, which demonstrates some sign of struggle to finance, but, at the same time, provides proof that companies financed through loans and credit cards could still scale up to millions of dollars of revenue. In addition, families and business acquaintances provided support.

Table 5.4   Financial sources of Inc. *companies nationwide*

Sources	Count	Share
Personal savings	322	67.2%
Personal or business loans	248	51.8%
Personal or business credit card	163	34.0%
Family	100	20.9%
Business acquaintances	57	11.9%
Angel investors	37	7.7%
Close friends	36	7.5%
Venture capitalists	31	6.5%
Government grants	18	3.8%
Have not used any finance before	65	13.6%
Sub-total	479	

Source: Authors' survey, conducted with Jared Konzcal.

Compared to those sources, the number of companies financed by angel investors and VCs was relatively small.

5.4   CHAPTER SUMMARY

The analysis of companies that received the Arch Grants demonstrated the process of starting companies and the surrounding environment for entrepreneurs. As we observed in the case of 1 Million Cups in Kansas City, entrepreneurs in St. Louis highly valued the peer-based learning between other recipients of Arch Grants. They exchanged information and provided feedback about a wide range of matters: from how to reformulate the business idea, how to interact with pro-bono lawyers be an entrepreneur, how to recruit and fire employees, that is, how to be an entrepreneur, to specific software coding techniques and marketing methods, such as expertise acquisition. This peer-based learning took place between entrepreneurs in the same sector, as well as other sectors, indicating that some of the core knowledge required for entrepreneurs was applicable to any kinds of entrepreneurs, and this feedback mechanism was intersectoral.

Moreover, despite the relatively compact size of St. Louis with its core area of about 10 square miles, the interaction between entrepreneurs took place at specific locations: primarily at the T-Rex building where a number of startup companies and support organizations co-existed, and the CORTEX area where several biomedical facilities, support organizations, and companies were located. The high interaction became possible through the frequent encounters and the proximity of as close as across the halls.

Lastly, the effective support environment was a product of constant and strategic co-ordination between support organizations in the area. Such connections were needed because support organizations monitored the development, as well as struggles, of startup companies and had to provide matching supports and referrals based on the evolution of companies. Additionally, those connections between support organizations enhanced a due diligence of supported companies; what they were advised in the past and how well they responded in the process.

The high-growth *Inc.* company interviews provided more understandings about the development process of companies, and their required inputs and resources. First, the high-growth companies established and expanded their businesses based on a clear market niche, that is, specific demands not met in the market or that other competitors could not substitute better. Many firms used IT or medical technologies, but few reported the use of or need for cutting-edge technologies from university research. Rather, entrepreneurs assembled available technologies for their market niche. This is a marked contrast to the dominant view that novelty in technology would enable new markets and businesses.

Second, in the course of firm development, many companies faced challenges and reoriented to substantial degrees. When such "pivots" took place, entrepreneurs noted that they were helped by other people, namely successful local entrepreneurs or other individuals who served as formal or informal mentors. This finding matches the survey result in which companies reported the importance of innovative people or ideas as well as the availability of mentors.

Third, many companies started small and scaled up incrementally yet successfully. Here, bootstrapping was a commonly observed method. Often, the startup capital was small or modest, from zero to five digits or up to $200,000, and entrepreneurs used their own savings, loans, credit cards, and friends and family circles, that is, ordinary capital sources around them. They ran business conservatively, yet were able to scale up to revenues of millions of dollars. A good number of entrepreneurs expressed their desire to control ownership of their companies and did not seek external equity investment, such as from VCs. In one case, the entrepreneur recalled that VCs approached the company because the company was growing rapidly, hinting that VCs might accelerate the growth, but the VCs' roles were not exactly as agents to create the growth.

Last but not least, the high-growth companies considered the availability of talent in the region to be very high. They did not express the need for specific coding, IT, or scientific skills, but rather for people with high aptitude. More specifically, they recruited young, smart, and curious recent college graduates and trained them rigorously to acquire specific skills needed for the companies. On some occasions, entrepreneurs described such talent as "go-getters," people who wanted to make a difference in a small company or did not need micromanagement. In short, the mentality of the talent was the factor for recruitment by high-growth companies, not specific technical skills or STEM background. Local universities contributed well to producing such talent. High-growth companies in these two regions recruited from major research universities in the vicinity, the University of MissouriKansas City, the University of Kansas, Washington University in St. Louis, St. Louis University, as well as from universities outside the metropolitan area, including Kansas State University, as far as 120 miles west of Kansas City, and the University of Missouri–Columbia, about 100 miles from either Kansas City or St. Louis. Moreover, talent also came from other smaller local public and private universities. These findings complement Chapter 3 well, in which we found no correlations between the entrepreneurship rates and research activities at Research I universities, but did with the rate of college-educated workforce at the metropolitan level.

6. What information sources do entrepreneurs follow? Network analysis with Twitter data

6.1 HOW THE TWITTER ANALYSIS WAS CONDUCTED[1]

Previous chapters examined the local ecosystems of entrepreneurship with several kinds of data: from nationwide regression analysis to regionwide surveys and qualitative interviews. In this chapter we shift gears to explore Twitter data. More specifically, we investigate what information sources entrepreneurs follow in Twitter.

This Twitter analysis has the advantage of identifying specific names of people and organizations serving as information sources for entrepreneurs. In Chapter 4, which covered Kansas City, the survey showed that entrepreneurs value informal access to innovative people, supportive local entrepreneurship support organizations, access to local business services, and mentors who give advice, among others. However, those are generic categories without specific names. Similarly, the story about 1 Million Cups provided analysis about how entrepreneurs mingled and what they found valuable from the interaction, but without identifying specific sources. The open-access nature of Twitter allows us to see specific connections between entrepreneurship-related tweeters and followers.

In addition, Twitter analysis can examine the local ecosystems at a larger regional scale in both Kansas City and St. Louis. Chapter 5, which featured St. Louis, provided a network map with support organizations, such as Arch Grants, ITEN, the Skandalaris Center at Washington University, and T-REX (an incubator), but those were still only a handful of organizations. Although we conducted surveys and interviews in transparent and systematic ways, the samples of

---

[1]   This chapter was written with Stephan Goetz and Yicheol Han.

our surveys and interviews were still small, hundreds and dozens, respectively. A resulting limitation is that it is hard to know how representative such resources and networks are within the region. In contrast, the Twitter platform gives us an advantage of sampling at the scale of hundreds of entrepreneurship support organizations and hundreds of thousands of their followers, thus radically expanding the scope of entrepreneurial activities in the region.

The challenge here was to identify entrepreneurship-oriented Twitter accounts among any kinds of Twitter accounts. In order to maximize our list of support organizations for each region, we compiled Twitter accounts from four sources. First, we collected information about organizations registered under StartupGenome. co.[2] Startup Genome was a nonprofit website aiming to collect and curate entrepreneurs and supporters at the regional level. In September 2014, we extracted all organizations, individuals, and events that they classified as accelerators, incubators, community enablers, academics, events, and service providers, which generated 45 entries for Kansas City and 88 entries for St. Louis.

Second, we used the Resource Navigator from KCSourceLink,[3] whose objective is to connect "nonprofit resource organizations that provide business-building services for small businesses." In essence, this is a free referral service for small businesses and entrepreneurs for a variety of support services, such as business planning, financial, legal, regulatory, tax, and technical services. This is a widely accessed resource organization for all kinds of entrepreneurs; for instance, they had 2,478 requests for service assistance, 5,270 online searches, and 238,804 web sessions in 2016 (interview with Maria Meyers and Kate Hodel, January 30, 2017). This navigator returned 254 sources for Kansas City. As KCSourceLink expanded its operation, they established USSourceLink, as well as MOSourceLink for the whole state of Missouri. MOSourceLink provided a further 62 sources for the St. Louis region.

For the third source of Twitter accounts, we further supplemented our own search to identify entrepreneurship support organizations, individuals, and events by consulting active local entrepreneurship supporters who were organizers and facilitators in Kauffman

---

[2]   Unfortunately, this organization was merged into Startup Compass, and the data is no longer openly accessible.

[3]   See KCSourceLink (2017).

Foundation's 1 Million Cups in Kansas City and St. Louis. As described in Chapter 4, 1 Million Cups serves as a go-to place for entrepreneurs and wannabe entrepreneurs, and those organizers connect and collaborate extensively with local entrepreneurship support organizations and individuals.

At that point, the three data sources identified 319 sources in Kansas City and 170 sources in St. Louis. Some of those organizations do not have Twitter accounts, and we had to remove duplicates, resulting in 168 sources for Kansas City and 87 for St. Louis.

Finally, in addition to local sources, we added national or international sources for entrepreneurs. We identified popular entrepreneurship-related Twitter accounts by tracing five sources, such as Huffington Post (2011,"The 8 best entrepreneurs to follow on Twitter"), Under30CEO (2011, "25 Twitter chats every entrepreneur must know"), Nibletz (2011, "50 startup related Twitter accounts to follow"), NextWeb (2011, "25 most influential people tweeting about entrepreneurship"), and Mashable (2009, "10 essential entrepreneurs to follow on Twitter"). These lists generated 130 accounts, excluding three that overlapped with the ones we already identified in the three local lists of Kansas City and St. Louis.[4]

With these local and national sources, we extracted all the followers of these Twitter accounts through SocialBro (now Audiense. com) between December 2014 and January 2015. This sampling generated a total of 110,350 followers for the region of Kansas City and 63,729 for St. Louis.[5] Missing data due to nonresponse can be problematic for network analysis (Doreian and Woodard 1992; Kossinets 2006; Lyles 2015); however, the open-access nature of Twitter allows us to analyze only a small portion of the sample (less than 3 percent). In the following sections, we analyze which Twitter accounts entrepreneurs follow and how we can categorize different Twitter followers.

---

[4] The ones that overlapped were @KauffmanFDN, @TechCocktail (now TechCoHQ), and @UPGlobalHQ.
[5] Here, we excluded the followers of national-only sources, because they were out of scope for our regional analysis, and their numbers were in the millions. For example, the most popular national one, @aplusk (Ashton Kutcher), was followed by over 16 million, and the majority of followers were outside our two analysis regions.

6.2 GENERAL TWITTER FOLLOWING PATTERNS

The different Twitter accounts related to entrepreneurship can be categorized into 11 groups. Table 6.1 presents those categories and share of the total.

Academic accounts (6.8 percent) are university-related ones. Associations (12.2 percent) are industry or trade associations, such as local chambers of commerce. Entrepreneurship support organizations (ESOs, 19.8 percent) are nonprofit organizations with a mission to promote entrepreneurship. We distinguish these ESOs from nonprofits (4.6 percent) whose mission is broader than entrepreneurship, such as Partnership for Downtown St. Louis and Downtown Council of Kansas City. In contrast to nonprofits, service providers (8.7 percent) help entrepreneurs, but in a for-profit business format. Events (3.8 percent share of the total) are the ones dedicated to entrepreneurship, and they may not necessarily be organizations; for example, Startup Weekend, its successor UP Global (bought by Techstars in June 2015), and Global Entrepreneurship Week.

Table 6.1 Types of Twitter accounts

Types	Kansas City	St. Louis	National	Subtotal	Total share
Academic	13	12		25	6.8%
Association	39	6		45	12.2%
Company	6	3	4	13	3.5%
Entrepreneur			93	93	25.3%
ESO	32	27	19	73*	19.8%
Event	10	1	3	14	3.8%
Government	24	4	4	29*	7.9%
Media	1		9	10	2.7%
Nonprofits	13	4		17	4.6%
Service providers	6	27		32*	8.7%
Other	15	1	1	17	4.6%
Subtotal	153	76	129	368	100.0%

Notes: *   Some Twitter accounts are run by organizations operating in both Kansas City and St. Louis, so the numbers do not add up in the subtotal. ESO stands for entrepreneurship support organization.

Table 6.2   The five most followed entrepreneur and media accounts

Entrepreneur		Media	
Accounts	Followers	Accounts	Followers
@aplusk	16,572,759	@HBRexchange	53,354
@mcuban	2,639,151	@TheSocialCMO	43,337
@biz	2,320,832	@Under30CEO	42,114
@ev	1,763,858	@journchat	9,760
@GuyKawasaki	1,439,099	@smckc	8,778

There is a major difference between the Twitter accounts of national and regional sources. In contrast to regional sources, the identified national accounts were heavily oriented to entrepreneurs (93 accounts). Those national accounts primarily belong to celebrity entrepreneurs, such as @aplusk (Ashton Kutcher), @mcuban (Mark Cuban), @ev (Ev Williams), and @GuyKawasaki (Guy Kawasaki). Christopher Isaac "Biz" Stone, the cofounder of Twitter, runs @biz. These accounts are followed by millions of Twitter users nationally.

Most of the media accounts come from our national list, but attract a smaller number of followers. The most followed ones were @HBRexchange (Harvard Business Review Exchange), @TheSocialCMO (Social Chief Marketing Officer), @Under30CEO (Under 30 CEO), and @journchat (a chat platform that was popular for journalists and industry public relations). There was one local media source – @smckc – the Social Media Club of Kansas City, a regional chapter of the Social Media Club that became the most active chapter nationally.

The five next most frequent categories are the ESOs (19.8 percent), associations (12.2 percent), service providers (8.9 percent), government (7.9 percent), and academic (6.8 percent). First, ESOs are the second largest category after entrepreneurs (25.3 percent). Table 6.3 lists the five most followed ESO accounts within the national, Kansas City, and St. Louis sources. The Case Foundation is run by Steve Case, the founder of AOL. The funds called 500 Startups, Y Combinator, and Techstars are nationally known so-called accelerators, where entrepreneurs get two to three months of training. The top five national accounts attract hundreds of thousands of followers. The ones in Kansas City are the Kauffman Foundation, its branch Kauffman Labs, Think Big Partners,

Table 6.3 The five most followed ESO accounts

| National | | Kansas City | | St. Louis | |
Accounts	Followers	Accounts	Followers	Accounts	Followers
@CaseFoundation	505,787	@KauffmanFDN	55,697	@ArchGrants	4,374
@500Startups	268,938	@KauffmanLabs	11,435	@DowntownTREX	3,911
@ycombinator	211,892	@ThinkBigKC	11,142	@CtrforEmergingTech	3,900
@AngelList	166,597	@IThinkBigger	9,513	@CapInnovators	2,702
@techstars	155,266	@KCSV	8,073	Lab 1500	2,670

Table 6.4   The five most followed association accounts in Kansas City and St. Louis

Kansas City		St. Louis	
Accounts	Followers	Accounts	Followers
Greater Kansas City Chamber	11,132	Application Developers Alliance	11,583
Lawrence Chamber	2,482	St. Louis Regional Chamber	6,458
Lee's Summit Chamber	1,842	World Trade Center St. Louis	846
Olathe Chamber	1,583	Grace Hill Women's Business Center	843
Grandview Chamber	1,379	Hispanic Chamber of STL	469

its branch Thinking Bigger, and KC Startup Village (@KCSV). The last one was originally a house in which several startup companies were located when Google Fiber first opened up in 2010. That house evolved into the KC Startup Village by expanding to a few blocks with a concentration of startup companies. The Kauffman Foundation is an organization rooted in Kansas City but with a national presence, and it attracted more than 50,000 followers during the studied period, while other Kansas City accounts had 8,000–11,000 followers.

In contrast, the accounts based in St. Louis attracted a substantially smaller number of followers, in the lower thousands. Those accounts are Arch Grants (a regional startup fund discussed in Chapter 5), T-REX (an incubator), Center for Emerging Technologies, Capital Innovators (an accelerator), and Lab 1500 (a co-working space that closed in 2015).

Second, associations include local or regional chambers of commerce or other business/industry associations, shown in Table 6.4. In Kansas City, the Greater Kansas City Chamber of Commerce is the largest regional chapter and attracts more than 11,000 followers. Other regional chapters, such as of Lawrence, Lee's Summit, Olathe, and Grandview, are substantially smaller in proportion to the population of each local area. St. Louis presents a different mixture of associations: Application Developers Alliance was the most followed account, followed by St. Louis Regional Chamber. The numbers for the other three associations, World Trade Center of St. Louis, Grace Hill Women's Business Center, and Hispanic Chamber of St. Louis, are substantially smaller with only hundreds of followers.

Table 6.5   The five most followed service providers in Kansas City and St. Louis

Kansas City		St. Louis	
Accounts	Followers	Accounts	Followers
Dr. Dave Computer Repair	1,462	LinkedSelling	7,207
Cremalab	1,086	Do314	6,500
Ariel Media	676	David Strom Inc.	4,747
Full Stack (formerly Cramer Dev)	485	Preservation Research Office	4,349
Stone Carlie & Company	383	Spoke Marketing	2,949

Third, service providers differ between Kansas City and St. Louis, as shown in Table 6.5. In St. Louis, the most followed accounts were Linked Selling (a business-to-business service), Do314 (a platform for announcing local music, art, and other events), David Strom (a business journalist), Preservation Research Office (a local historic building preservation consulting company), and Spoke Marketing (a marketing service provider). All of these accounts have thousands of followers. In contrast, the major accounts of this category in Kansas City have fewer followers, in lower thousands or hundreds: Dr. Dave Computer Repair, Cremalab (a web design service), Ariel Media (a branding and marketing agency), Full Stack (a software developing service), and Stone Carlie (an accounting office). With the exception of Stone Carlie, operating in both St. Louis and Kansas City, these service provider accounts are heterogeneous between the two cities. Moreover, while St. Louis had ESO accounts with a smaller number of followers than Kansas City, St. Louis has more active for-profit service providers in the region.

Fourth, there are three different kinds of government accounts, as shown in Table 6.6. At the national level, the Small Business Administration and Department of Commerce are highly relevant for running businesses and followed by six-digit numbers of people. The next most popular accounts were the Social Security Administration and the General Service Administration's branch, Office of Small Business Utilization, but with substantially smaller number of followers.

In Kansas City, Kansas City Area Development Council, Kansas Department of Agriculture, and Mid-America Manufacturing

Table 6.6   The most followed government accounts in the USA, Kansas City, and St. Louis

National		Kansas City		St. Louis	
Accounts	Followers	Accounts	Followers	Accounts	Followers
@SBAgov	142,223	KC Area Development Council	6,492	St. Louis Public Library	6,737
US Dept of Commerce	127,163	KS Dept. of Agriculture	5,320	MO Secretary of State	3,047
Social Security Admin	18,962	Mid-America Manuf. Tech Center	3,143	MO Dept. of Natural Resources	2,873
GSA Small Business Utilization	4,142			MO Dept. of Agriculture	2,572
				MO Dept. of Labor	2,066

Table 6.7   The most followed academic accounts

Kansas City		St. Louis	
Accounts	Followers	Accounts	Followers
Missouri Western Univ. Small Business Inst	3,738	Donald Danforth Plant Science Center	5,341
Metropolitan CC, Inst for Workforce Innovation	1,915	Center for Nanoscience, Univ of MO, St. Louis	4,130
Johnson County CC, Center for Business & Tech	1,420	SLU Community and Econ. Development Clinic	2,465
KU Center for Technology Commercialization	1,337	Maryville Univ. Adult Undergraduate & Graduate Studies	2,449
UMKC Small Business & Tech Development Center	1,000	Skandalaris Center for Entrepreneurial Studies, WashU	2,146

Technology Centers were most followed, and in St. Louis, the St. Louis Public Library was most followed. There are several branches of the Missouri state government, such as Secretary of State, Departments of Natural Resources, Agriculture, and Labor, which were followed by both St. Louis and Kansas City Twitter users.

Lastly, the academic category consists of university-related Twitter accounts (Table 6.7). In Kansas City, the most followed accounts were from smaller universities, such as the Small Business Institute at Missouri Western University, the Institute for Workforce Innovation at Metropolitan Community College (CC), and the Center for Business and Technology at Johnson County Community College. Then, two accounts from larger universities came next: the Center for Technology Commercialization at the University of Kansas (KU) and the Small Business and Technology Development Center at University of Missouri, Kansas City (UMKC).

While the top Kansas City accounts were business administration oriented, the two most followed Twitter accounts in St. Louis were science oriented: The Donald Danforth Plant Science Center and the Center for Nanoscience at the University of Missouri, St. Louis. Then, business-related accounts came next: the Community and Economic Development Clinic at St. Louis University (SLU), the Adult Undergraduate and Graduate Studies program at Maryville

University, and the Skandalaris Center for Entrepreneurial Studies at Washington University (WashU).

6.3 COMMUNITY DETECTION IN EACH REGION

Next, we analyzed these 368 Twitter accounts to determine which communities they can be classified in. This is based on the mathematics of social network analysis, employing the natural cluster method with the yED program (Girvan and Newman 2002). This analysis reveals some forms of communities of Twitter accounts; for example, people who follow X account also tend to follow Y, Z, and other accounts. In addition, this analysis allows us to find different kinds of communities of Twitter accounts even within a region.

Kansas City

Of 110,350 followers in Kansas City, we identified seven different communities, as shown in Figure 6.1. Not surprisingly, most communities are location based, which demonstrates a highly localized nature of Twitter following. Except for three accounts (2 percent), all other accounts are grouped into national, Kansas City-, or St. Louis-based communities. First, the national-source accounts are grouped into two communities: National 1 consists of 23 accounts mostly with celebrity entrepreneurs often with millions of followers, as well as national government agencies, such as SBA and Department of Commerce, plus foundations like the Case Foundation. National 2 consists of 16 accounts more linked to entrepreneurship support activities, such as accelerators, Startup Weekend, Angel List, and some other entrepreneurs. Note that celebrity entrepreneurs in National 1 tweet on many general topics, while other entrepreneurs in National 2 tweet messages that are more directly relevant to entrepreneurship and events. These celebrity and more dedicated entrepreneurs demonstrate two different kinds of people or organizations to follow.

Second, the accounts based in Kansas City are grouped into three communities:

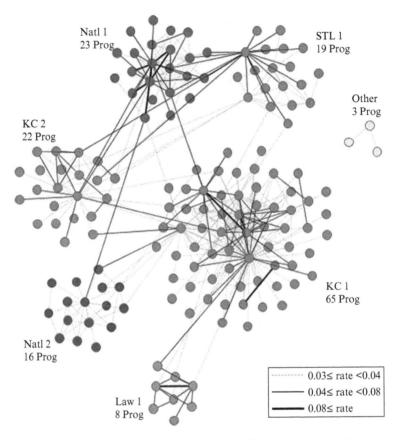

Figure 6.1   Twitter community map with followers in Kansas City

1. Kansas City 1 consists of 65 accounts from a variety of organizations, such as ESOs, companies, nonprofits, associations, and media.
2. Kansas City 2 consists of 22 programs from some entrepreneurs, ESOs, governments, and academic accounts.
3. In addition, there are eight small programs based in Lawrence, Kansas.

This separation of Lawrence accounts again suggests the localized nature of Twitter. Lawrence is about 45 miles west of Kansas City, forming a different entrepreneurial community. Moreover, the

Table 6.8 Selected accounts in two national communities

National 1			National 2		
Accounts	Category	Followers	Accounts	Category	Followers
@aplusk	Entrepreneur	16,572,759	@500Startups	ESO	268,938
@mcuban	Entrepreneur	2,639,151	davemcclure	Entrepreneur	255,927
@biz	Entrepreneur	2,320,832	@ycombinator	ESO	211,892
@ev	Entrepreneur	1,763,858	ericries	Entrepreneur	200,611
garyvee	Entrepreneur	1,113,645	msuster	Entrepreneur	188,125
SteveCase	Entrepreneur	702,774	@AngelList	ESO	166,597
@CaseFoundation	Nonprofit	505,787	@techstars	ESO	155,266
@SmallBizLady	Entrepreneur	281,285	bhorowitz	Entrepreneur	141,481
@SBAgov	Government	142,223	sgblank	Entrepreneur	126,608
Dept of Commerce	Government	127,163	StartupWeekend	ESO	120,142

separation of two communities within Kansas City suggests that there are two different kinds of followers or entrepreneurs. The Twitter accounts for Kansas City 1 seem to represent more mainstream entrepreneurship sources; media and other key stakeholders in Kansas City often speak about entrepreneurship organizations and events. For Kansas City 2, Marketing Profs LLC is based in Kansas City, but it had more than 272,000 nationally based followers (see Table 6.9). Beyond that, a smaller number of a very different kind of entrepreneurs followed specialized government, academic, and other ESO accounts in the area. For example, FastTrac is an entrepreneurship program operated by Kauffman Foundation, but its participants are small-scale businesses and first-time entrepreneurs in contrast to the accounts for entrepreneurs who aim to grow quickly in Kansas City 1. Similarly, Pipeline in Kansas City 2 is a program dedicated to entrepreneurs who have been operating a business, have annual revenue of about $1 million, and aim to expand to the next stage. Note that these Twitter accounts are a mixture of organizations, individuals, and events (often hosted by a handful of key organizers), which do not warrant individual accounts. For instance, 1 Million Cups in Kansas City, extensively discussed in Chapter 4, does not own its own Twitter account, but is hosted by staff of the Kauffman Foundation (@KauffmanFDN).

St. Louis

We identified 63,729 Twitter users in St. Louis. Again, most accounts are location-based, but we find more divided communities within each region of Kansas City and St. Louis. Here, national accounts were all in one group, National 1, which includes celebrity entrepreneurs, more dedicated entrepreneurs, ESOs, and governments.

The Twitter accounts in St. Louis are grouped into three communities (Table 6.10). St. Louis 1 is the largest of the three with 65 accounts, and they include public or semi-public organizations, such as Partnership for Downtown St. Louis, St. Louis Public Library, and St. Louis Regional Chamber. Do314 is an organization which provides event information in St. Louis. Then, a number of ESOs that we learned about from Arch Grants companies in Chapter 5 are listed: T-REX, Center for Emerging Technologies, Capital Innovators, ITEN, BioSTL, and so on. One exception is the Skandalaris Center for Entrepreneurship at Washington University,

Table 6.9 Selected accounts in two Kansas City communities

	Kansas City 1			Kansas City 2	
Accounts	Types	Followers	Accounts	Types	Followers
@KauffmanFDN	ESO	55,697	@MarketingProfs	Entrepreneur	272,066
Google Fiber	Company	40,225	@ThinkBigKC	ESO	11,142
Downtown Council of KC	Nonprofit	16,869	Kansas Dept of Agriculture	Government	5,320
Farm to Table Kitchen	Company	14,216	FastTrac	ESO	3,496
@KauffmanLabs	ESO	11,435	MO Secretary of State	Government	3,047
KC Chamber of Commerce	Association	11,132	Pipeline	ESO	2,058
@smckc	Media	8,778	Johnson County CC	Academic	1,420
SourceLink Events	Event	8,576	Workforce Solutions Group	Academic	762
@KCSV	ESO	8,073	KU Bioscience & Tech Center	Academic	523
KC Development Council	Government	6,492	St. Louis CC	Academic	208

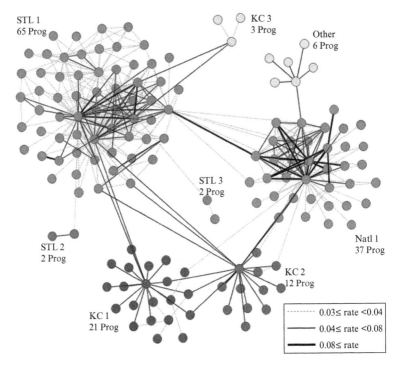

Figure 6.2   Twitter network maps with followers in St. Louis

which is grouped in St. Louis 3 along with the Twitter account of the entrepreneurship courses of Washington University. In contrast, St. Louis 2 has two accounts related to St. Louis University: one communicating about its entrepreneurship courses and the other of the Billiken Angels, which invests in the greater St. Louis region but has strong ties to alumni of St. Louis University.

6.4   SUMMARY

The Twitter analysis in this chapter illuminates the information sources and network patterns of entrepreneurs from a different angle. By identifying 87 active Twitter accounts in St. Louis and 168 accounts in Kansas City, as well as tens to hundreds of thousands of followers in each region, we can analyze the connections within the

Table 6.10 Selected Twitter accounts in three St. Louis communities

	St. Louis 1			St. Louis 2		
Accounts	Types	Followers	Accounts	Types	Followers	
Downtown STL	Nonprofit	28,041	SLU entrepreneurship	Academic	2,047	
LinkedSelling	Service provider	7,207	Billiken Angels	ESO	1,030	
St. Louis Public Library	Government	6,737				
Do314	Service provider	6,500				
St. Louis Regional Chamber	Association	6,458				
Danforth Plant Science Center	Academic	5,341		St. Louis 3		
@ArchGrants	ESO	4,374				
@DowntownTREX	ESO	3,911	Accounts	Types	Followers	
@CtrforEmergingTech	ESO	3,900	Skandalaris Center, WashU	Academic	2,146	
@CapInnovators	ESO	2,702	WashU entrepreneurship	Academic	2,054	
Lab 1500	ESO	2,670				
ITEN	ESO	2,365				
Innovate St. Louis	ESO	2,363				
StartLouis	ESO	2,207				
Cultivation Capital	ESO	2,115				
BioSTL	ESO	1,990				

local system at a substantially larger scale. This is a new contribution to this topic, because previous academic studies on regional economies were able to identify network and information sources only aggregated into higher-level categories, such as industry associations, rival firms, chambers of commerce, universities, and suppliers (Porter 1998; Motoyama 2008; Motoyama et al. 2018).

While this Twitter analysis is novel, we need to be cautious that the number of followers per se does not become the most important element of analysis throughout the chapter. A Twitter account with 5,000 followers does not mean that it is more important than another with 4,000 followers. This caution applies particularly when we discuss national accounts that are followed by millions of people, and we cannot compare and analyze the importance of national vis-à-vis regional accounts. Having said that, differences in the numbers of Twitter followers can reveal important aspects if we compare accounts in the same regional setting. For example, the Kauffman Foundation was followed by more than 55,000 people during December 2014 through January 2015, while the Bioscience and Technology Center at the University of Kansas was followed by only 523 people, which tells us that the latter is not likely a major player in the local system of entrepreneurship. Combined with the analysis of community classification, we can see that the Bioscience and Technology Center attracts a very different kind of people from the Kauffman Foundation, because the Bioscience and Technology Center belongs to a different subset of community within Kansas City. Moreover, we can analyze still other features about the Twitter following patterns by categorizing groups and analyzing within groups.

The first major finding is the localized nature of the entrepreneurship system. In other words, active Twitter accounts – and hence entrepreneurship-related organizations and events – vary substantially between Kansas City and St. Louis. There are few organizations that were frequently followed in the two cities, with the exception of the two chambers of commerce in the regions. In Kansas City, people follow a variety of organizations: ESOs (Kauffman Foundation, KC Startup Village), companies (Google Fiber, Farm to Table Kitchen), nonprofits (Downtown Council), media (Social Media Club), events (SourceLink), and government agencies (Development Council).

In contrast, the most followed accounts in St. Louis were primarily a couple of highly active for-profit service providers (LinkedSelling and Do314); the majority of the rest were ESOs. There are other kinds of accounts in the government category, such as St. Louis Public Library under government, but this differs from the state government branches identified in Kansas City. There is also one academic organization, the Danforth Plant Science Center, but its scientific nature is very different from most other business-oriented academic organizations in St. Louis.

Second, we find that interviews of Arch Grants recipients and this Twitter analysis identified overlapping support organizations. Those organizations are T-REX (an incubator), Center for Emerging Technologies, Capital Innovators (an accelerator), Lab 1500, ITEN, Innovate St. Louis, Start Louis (a site for startup-related events), and Cultivation Capital (a VC firm). These ESOs are highly active on Twitter.

Third, the analysis for community classification revealed different kinds of entrepreneurship communities and associated followers even within each region. Moreover, these divisions of communities differ between Kansas City and St. Louis. With two communities detected in Kansas City, one seems to be a mainstream group led by the Kauffman Foundation, Google Fiber, KC Sourcelink, and KC Startup Village, among others. The other community consists of support services (Think Big Partners, Pipeline), the state governments of both Kansas and Missouri, and academic institutions. Overall, the number of followers is substantially smaller for this second group, only in the lower thousands or even the hundreds. This suggests that entrepreneurs in the second group are at different stages or specific orientations and rely more on specialized support services.

In St. Louis, the division between the three communities is based on university lines: the first and mainstream one mentioned just above, the second one based on Washington University (the Skandalaris Center and entrepreneurship courses), and the third one based on St. Louis University.

We need to keep in mind that this Twitter analysis is one of several methods to analyze local entrepreneurship systems that are highly complex, and no single type of data can describe the whole. The Twitter data uses the largest samples in each region, and its open-access nature allows few missing tweeters and followers, but it is not a comprehensive one, either. For instance, the survey and interviews in the previous chapters demonstrated the importance of mentors, but mentorship is an ad hoc and individual relationship between a mentor and mentee, not necessarily like forming a Twitter-based relationship or a mentor followed by hundreds or thousands of mentees. In fact, those business mentors are often successful, rich, and extremely busy entrepreneurs who prefer the less public attention they find on Twitter. Similarly, there may be other hidden yet important entrepreneurship supporters and players in the Twitterverse.

In addition, this Twitter analysis does not comment on the quality of information transacted via Twitter, and we do not intend to argue that entrepreneurs get new business ideas through tweets or that the accounts with larger numbers of followers disseminate more innovative ideas. Our intention here is simply to identify potential information sources and active regional players, and this Twitter analysis can add another layer to our understanding.

7. Conclusion: Beyond innovation to an entrepreneurship model

7.1 INTRODUCTION

In Chapter 1, we started with a tale of two entrepreneurs, Joe Anderson with patented nanotechnology, and Charlie Hopp, a casual entrepreneur, and presented our bold hypothesis that a casual entrepreneur was more likely to succeed. The following chapters examined entrepreneurship from various angles: In Chapters 3 to 6, we analyzed entrepreneurship in Kansas City and St. Louis using surveys, interviews, and Twitter analysis. The companies we interviewed included startup companies of Arch Grants and 1MC, as well as high-growth firms. In addition, we employed nationwide quantitative data in Chapter 2 to analyze entrepreneurship rates from three different sources of data: Business Dynamics Statistics from the US Census Bureau for all industry startups, National Establishment Time Series data for high-tech startups, and the Inc. 5000 list of fastest-growing firms. Lacking a single perfect database of entrepreneurship activities, it was our attempt to use different kinds of data and methods to examine entrepreneurship from multiple perspectives to present a fuller picture. Findings from each section and chapter of this book present a somewhat cohesive picture of entrepreneurial activities and local systems. The paths of entrepreneurship, including those by successful high-growth entrepreneurs, are substantially closer to the one by Charlie Hopp, while the current theory of innovation and practice seems to primarily support Joe Anderson. The purpose of this final chapter is to synthesize all those findings and explain why a casual entrepreneur is more likely to succeed. Then, we induce the theory of entrepreneurship, and provide policy and practice implications.

7.2   FINDING HIGHLIGHTS

Level 1: Individual and Entrepreneur Level

Entrepreneurship is a risky business with major reorientation

We organize our findings at two broad levels, individual-company and regional levels. First, at the individual-company level, entrepreneurship is a risky business with many bumps on the road. We observed that many companies experienced major evolutions of their businesses or sometimes faced "pivots," a complete reorientation. Such bumps or evolution were present in both startup and high-growth companies. The recipients of the Arch Grants were, by definition, winners of the business plan competition, meaning that a panel of judges regarded their business models highly. However, it did not mean that simply executing the business plan would make each company successful. Each company had to go through substantial improvements or major reorientation of the business plan and other aspects of running the business.

We observed those changes even for more developed Inc. 5000 high-growth firms with millions of dollars of revenue. Among experienced entrepreneurs, one had run two companies before, yet he described how the types of clients shifted quickly when starting his third business. Their alumni database business initially targeted local education districts, but soon they had to reorient to private high schools and universities. Moreover, the philosophy of this entrepreneur was to make every employee go, sit, and observe how their clients were using their technology. Otherwise, they would be quickly left behind in the market (Business Service Company A).

Keep in mind that the companies we analyzed have a heavy selection bias: All of the companies were surviving and often successful companies; thus, we did not interview companies that had ceased to exist. As mentioned in Chapter 1, there is a 5-50 rule: 50 percent of companies cease to exist after five years. This fact only magnifies the risky reality of entrepreneurship. The Small Business Administration periodically publishes the survival rate of all businesses in the USA, and the general pattern is that one-third of employer firms exit after two years, and one-half of those firms exit after five years (SBA 2012).

Arch Grants firms tended to perform better than the national average: 95 percent of firms survive after 1.5 years and 73 percent after 2.5 years (Arch Grants 2014). Even among the Inc. 5000 firms, many changes happen after ten years – 11 percent are acquired (for successful or unsuccessful reasons), 1.6 percent no longer exist, and 11 percent of firms are unknown, possibly ceased to exist (Rice et al. 2017).

This is the harsh reality of the entrepreneurship world, which our entrepreneurial development model and support system is intended to reflect. Regardless of the quality of their business plans or their past success, some companies fail no matter what, and entrepreneurship is a probability business. We should expect some failure rate and let some companies go, or, in fact, let them fail fast so that those failed entrepreneurs can try the next round of business with their lessons learned. Picking winners is extremely difficult, and letting the company survive should not be the goal of the support system. We revisit this issue in Section 7.4 on policy recommendations.

Entrepreneurs have to learn
Entrepreneurs have to learn how to start and run businesses. There are so many different kinds of skills and knowledge that entrepreneurs must acquire, and there is no such thing as a born genius entrepreneur who knows everything about it. The interactions between Arch Grants recipients and the information they exchanged were good examples. They exchanged knowledge about how to be an entrepreneur, such as how to reformulate business ideas, what type of funding might suit a company best, how to interact with pro-bono lawyers, and how to select the first few employees (Motoyama and Knowlton 2016). There was more nitty-gritty knowledge about how to register your company, what can be taxed, how not to be taxed, how to find local zoning codes to figure out where you can locate your business, and so on. One entrepreneur noted that each of them was in a different business, but the same thought processes coursed through the cohort of Arch Grants recipients that benefited them from sharing (Biotech Firm B).

In addition to the general knowledge about being an entrepreneur and running a business, entrepreneurs exchanged specific expert and technical information. This could include information about coding particular software, developing the company's interactive website, or changing a product to make it more appealing to customers. Life science companies among the Arch Grants recipients started to organize an informal group to study the application of SBIR grants by the federal government and provide feedback to each other (Biotech Firm A).

Moreover, this learning in entrepreneurship is a developmental process in which what entrepreneurs learn differs according to the stage of their businesses over a long time, such as years. One presenter at 1MC remarked that what you were doing 16 months ago and what you would be doing in three years were not the same skills (Entrepreneur D).

In short, there are so many different and detailed kinds of knowledge that no single textbook or university course can teach them all. Entrepreneurs did not know what problems or challenges they would face, and the only way to find out was by starting their businesses. In addition, the ways that entrepreneurs run businesses and become successful are so heterogeneous that there is no single right formula, either. Thus, this is experimental learning in which entrepreneurs have to start the process, identify issues, get hints from others, and apply the knowledge to their own businesses – that is, learning by doing.

The importance of peer- and mentor-based feedback and support organizations

The experimental learning primarily came from feedback from peer entrepreneurs and mentors, often experienced and senior entrepreneurs who have gone through similar entrepreneurial experiences before. The importance of this peer- and mentor-based feedback system can be seen in multiple forms of our data. First, with our survey, mentors that give advice (52.5 percent) were the most frequently cited source of new ideas for the company, ahead of other factors, such as customers and users (43.8 percent) and informal networks with other friends (42 percent). It is important to note that the primary emphasis of the conventional cluster theory was these suppliers, customers, and informal networks (Porter 1998), but researchers have not paid much attention to peer- and mentor-based feedback.

Second, entrepreneurs valued the learning from interacting and receiving feedback at 1MC. They loved receiving networking and learning opportunities from a set of panelists, as well as other audience members who asked questions and people who approached, questioned, and challenged them after the presentation event. Similarly, one of the most visible findings from the Arch Grants recipients was this peer-based learning. More than two-thirds of them highlighted the interaction with and learning from other recipients, and they described the benefits of the startup fund in St. Louis as "the great environment" (IT Firm A).

Third, entrepreneurs of high-growth *Inc.* companies also valued business mentors, and three-quarters of them cited such relationships. The nature of this mentor–mentee relationship varies substantially, including how mentees found their mentors, how often they met, and what advice they received. In some cases, mentors gave specific technical advice, such as on legal matters (Business Service Company C). In other cases, one mentor warned his mentee how much the company might be in trouble (Business Service Company E). Other topics included more general ones, such as how to focus, how to balance work and life, and how to communicate with employees.

Multiple circles of mentorships intersected at many points in the case of Kansas City. Ewing Marion Kauffman, a successful pharmaceutical entrepreneur and founder of the Kauffman Foundation, mentored a number of the next generation of entrepreneurs. One of his mentees, Barnett Helzberg of Helzberg Diamond, wanted to give back what Kauffman taught him and established a formal mentorship program, HEMP. One of the three founders of an Inc. 5000 firm, which we are calling Business Service Company F, participated in HEMP. Kauffman also mentored Neal Patterson, one of the founders of Cerner Corporation, a nationwide medical data system company, who subsequently mentored the entrepreneur of IT Company A. In addition, entrepreneurs encountered mentors from their previous jobs or industry experience. In St. Louis, one entrepreneur proudly explained that he had the good fortune to work at Apple in his early career, and reported that Steve Jobs was his inspiration and mentor.

In whatever way each entrepreneur found his or her mentor, it was evident that many entrepreneurs had mentors and valued them. This feeds back to the point that entrepreneurship is a learning process across stages. At the startup stage, the learning curve is very steep, and they had to learn everything about starting and running businesses. Even at the later stage, entrepreneurs still have to keep learning, because there are new problems emerging as their businesses reach a new stage, and their market keeps changing. Entrepreneurs need sources from which they can get advice and hints.

It is worth mentioning that these mentorships are long-term. The relationship often does not form instantly and can easily take months to develop. This is because some of the struggles that entrepreneurs are facing are their innermost problems, and they do not want to share externally or even internally with some of their employees or other founders. Sometimes, entrepreneurs do not admit that they are having some of the biggest problems (Helzberg, interview, December 18, 2012). Both the mentee and mentor have to develop trust in each other, which naturally takes time. One entrepreneur succinctly described that those entrepreneurs who can spill their guts benefit the most (Rush, interview, January 24, 2013).

These aspects about entrepreneurs' learning and mentorship lead to the fact that the whole process is not of one entrepreneur coming up with a question and his or her mentor giving an answer right away. As mentioned before, the challenges that entrepreneurs face are heterogeneous because each market is different, and each entrepreneur runs the company in a different way. Thus, the mentor is not the person who has a cache of answers, but he or she is the one who asks the right questions and guides the mentee in better directions. This has an important implication for the support system, which we will revisit in Section 7.4.

Identifying the niche market
The primary role of entrepreneurs is to identify a market niche with specific clients. The niche market can be between sectors or within a sector with a highly specific segment. For instance, Business Service Company J operated between the education and IT sectors, marketing educational software programs to superintendents of school districts. The primary market of IT Company B was between legal and IT sectors, developing an IT system for legal departments of large firms. Alternatively, a company may specialize in a highly defined segment within one sector. For example, IT Company A operated in the data and server maintenance business, and their core competence was the swift recovery of the IT system in Kansas City when the system unavoidably broke down a few times a year.

While the ways each entrepreneur identified the niche market were heterogeneous, they often gained some hints or insights from previous business experiences. The key was finding an underserved market where no other competitors provided a product or service. In addition, it was crucial that each entrepreneur knew who exactly would be paying at what price. Thus, this was a process of identifying specific clients, which could lead to a definite start of a business, not a typical marketing analysis involving categorizing a relatively large market segment, such as $1.5 trillion for the education market, and assuming or declaring the company's aim to capture 5 percent or even 1 percent of that market. Such marketing analysis was meaningless if the entrepreneur could not find a specific client paying for what he or she proposed. The goal was not to be Google or Facebook with hundreds of millions of users; a hedgehog with a small but clearly defined territory would be a better target.[1]

Many startup entrepreneurs that we observed through 1MC or Arch Grants had some ideas about the niche market they should target, but they were constantly refining their ideas. Every Inc. 5000 entrepreneur had a very clear idea about where their market was, who their competitors were, why others would not intrude in their niche market, or why they could provide better products or services.

It is important to note that this identification of niche market was usually not based on the use of cutting-edge or patented technologies. We sampled dozens of companies in so-called high-tech sectors, such as IT and health industries, yet the number using high technologies is extremely small. Only one company relied on patented technologies: Health Company A for its IT-based system for drug testing. Having said that, we admit that interviews and surveys can have a selection bias, and this small number itself is not the focus of the point here. Our intention here is to highlight that commercializing cutting-edge technologies is only one of many ways to establish a new business and market.

We would like to refer to the case of MIT and its entrepreneurship program here. As one of the top engineering and science schools in the world, its students often come up with business ideas and go to the Martin Center for Entrepreneurship for consultation. Bill Aulet, the managing director of the center, repeatedly observed the same pattern proposed by students and created a set of tips. Almost all business ideas were based on novelty of technologies and lacked the perspective of markets or clients (Aulet, interview, November

---

[1] The concept of identifying and capturing a niche market here is highly similar to the hedgehog concept introduced in *Good to Great* by Jim Collins (2001), who studied large companies with sustained revenue growth. Essentially, he argued that the hedgehog concept, an understanding about the core business where you are the best player, is one of the five features of great companies.

19, 2013). The fact that an invention can do this cool thing does not yield a successful business if no one pays for it. In his book *Disciplined Entrepreneurship* (2013), he addressed 24 steps to prepare for launching a new business, and essentially all of them are about marketing. This is to say that identifying a niche market and using cutting-edge technologies are not mutually exclusive, but the former is more important than the latter.

Power of incremental and internal growth

Entrepreneurs may start their company small, but they become able to scale up over the years. The Arch Grants recipients started with a modest $50,000, but that does not mean that many of them burned through cash in one year and quit. Earlier, we listed their good survival rate, 73 percent after two and a half years. In terms of annual revenue, those companies grew to be $368,000 after one and a half years and $779,000 after two and a half years, with a good level of variation between them (Arch Grants 2014).

The prevalence of self-finance and bootstrapping among the *Inc.* 5000 companies represented further evidence that companies could start small but grow to millions of dollars in annual revenue. As long as each company had its specific niche market and kept improving or finding more markets, that is, keeping off competitors, it could reach that scale of business and still achieve further growth. The median annual revenue growth of our interviewed *Inc.* firms was over 96 percent in both Kansas City and St. Louis (see Tables 5.2 and 5.3).

The fact that only two out of 32 Inc. 5000 companies (6.3 percent) received VC investment clearly signals that there are alternative ways to start and grow businesses successfully. We further confirmed with our survey that only 6.4 percent of 479 responding *Inc.* firms, nationally represented, used VC finance. Other financial sources included personal savings (67.2 percent), personal or business loans (51.8 percent), and personal or business credit cards (34.0 percent). In addition, our quantitative analysis in Chapter 3 demonstrated no statistical association between VC investment and startup or *Inc.* high-growth rates among metropolitan areas. Thus, even among companies with little VC investment, there can be a high concentration of high-growth firms.

Moreover, an interview from IT Company B gave a nuanced context to the topic of investment and company growth. It was not VC investment that induced the growth of the company, but the successful growth of the company attracted the eyes of VCs. They received two to three inquiries about possible investment from VC firms every week. This points out that VC is not necessarily an agent for growth and success, but rather its role is to make the growth faster or possibly larger. In other words, not receiving VC investment is not a hindrance to the birth or growth of successful businesses or regions.

Level 2: Regional Level

Importance of entrepreneurship support organizations (ESOs)

Next, we extend our finding about the learning feedback mechanism of entrepreneurs, which was at the individual level, to the regional level. While the peer- and mentor-based learning was present, no less important was the learning from ESOs. We observed many kinds of ESOs with different functions and target entrepreneurs or sectors. For instance, in St. Louis, ITEN focused on startup companies in the IT sector and provided pitching practice through their Mock Angel Program for one-on-one mentorship and organized events such as Second Thursday to create collusion between entrepreneurs. T-REX was an incubator providing business space for startups and also organizing workshops for skill improvement, such as computer programming. The Skandalaris Center at Washington University functioned to educate students about entrepreneurship, organized business plan competitions, and connected students to local startups through internships and other methods, such as letting startup entrepreneurs serve as judges for student competition events. Some organizations focused on specific sectors, such as bioscience, financial technology (FinTech), or manufacturing, while other organizations targeted women or all sectors. Table 5.1 listed about 35 of these support organizations in St. Louis.

Many of these organizations were nonprofit, while some were for-profit. Each organization usually had a handful of full-time staff and some part-time, meaning that the operation of each organization was relatively limited and focused on companies in the local area. In some cases of for-profit organizations, such as Cambridge Innovation Center, the headquarters operation was elsewhere, but the St. Louis branch operated semi-autonomously.

In Kansas City, we identified a similar number of support organizations. We note that some organizations had other kinds of specific foci; for example, the objective of KC SourceLink was to be a one-stop shop for any kind of entrepreneur to find resources in the area. The Pipeline Program recruited companies in the middle stage of development, created a cohort, provided monthly workshops, and matched them with mentors. This is because the organizer identified that companies with about $1 million in annual revenue often faced similar major problems with scaling up the organization (Cobb, interviews, January 17, 2014 and April 22, 2014). All these observations signify that the support system of entrepreneurship consists of a number of support organizations.

Local learning system
Throughout this book, it has become evident that the interactions of entrepreneurs with their peers, experienced mentors, and supporter organizations primarily took place at the local level, that is, they were located in the same metropolitan area. In addition, much of the learning and entrepreneurship vibe was happening through face-to-face interactions.

Earlier in this chapter, we mentioned that an Arch Grants recipient described the "great environment" for startups in St. Louis. She was explaining this environment as a context where she could ask questions of others, and "other people stop by and ask me things: what do you think about this idea?" (IT Firm A). The interaction was spontaneous and iterative among multiple entrepreneurs, which required people's presence in person.

An example from 1MC further reveals that this local interaction would not take place simply due to the presence of multiple entrepreneurs living in the same area. First-time entrepreneurs and wannabe entrepreneurs had to tap into resources and networks from scratch, which was not easy at all for some people. A presenter at 1MC noted that she did not have any meaningful connections before attending 1MC or identify useful programs, organizations, or events by herself. "It sounds very small, but it's not, because it's hard to develop that network" (Entrepreneur F). Of course, Kansas City had many entrepreneurship support organizations before the 2012 start of 1MC, but that did not necessarily mean that entrepreneurs knew where to go to interact or get information. Thus, these interactions required a specific entrepreneurship-related context, such as presenting business ideas and receiving feedback, and they took the form of periodic and open events visible to outsiders. In comparison, the story was different for Inc. 5000 list entrepreneurs who developed their personal connections over years through their businesses and described Kansas City as a small town with low social distance.

The local nature of interaction was also reflected in the high use of local Twitter accounts as information sources. We identified 87 active Twitter accounts related to entrepreneurship in St. Louis and another 168 accounts in Kansas City, and further extracted 63,729 and 110,350 followers in each city, respectively. We observed that the Twitter accounts followed by entrepreneurs in each city were highly complementary to the organizations and events we identified through interviews of 1MC presenters and Arch Grants recipients. Moreover, as the operation of most ESOs was primarily structured within a local area, the highly active and followed Twitter accounts differed substantially between Kansas City and St. Louis. In Kansas City, active players were the Kauffman Foundation, KC Startup Village, Downtown Council, and KCSourceLink, for example. In St. Louis, the active accounts were a couple of highly active for-profit service providers (LinkedSelling and Do314) and other support organizations, such as T-REX (an incubator), Center for Emerging Technologies, Capital Innovators (an accelerator), Lab1500, ITEN, Innovate St. Louis, Start Louis (a site for startup-related events), and Cultivation Capital (a venture capital firm).

Entrepreneurs cultivate a variety of sources
Through the long process of entrepreneurial development, entrepreneurs often received help from multiple organizations and individuals. Entrepreneurs found support, received advice, and got inspiration and hints through attending events, participating in formal programs, meeting with mentors, and so on. Two Arch Grants recipients noted this kind of chain of support: One of them received support from Capital Innovators, Missouri Technology Corporation, and ITEN (IT Firm D). The other one received support from ITEN, publicity in the local business journal, finding clients, and Capital Innovators (Other Firm C).

The need for multiple kinds of support from multiple organizations makes sense because, as described, entrepreneurs have to learn a number of skills, and need to improve or pivot on multiple fronts. Furthermore, those skills and changes will evolve over their entrepreneurial stages.

This means that a local entrepreneurship system must have a cluster of support organizations to complement a range of support functions. Moreover, the complementarity and range of supports are not organized with a simple division of functions; for instance, financial support from Organization A, pitching practice from Organization B, marketing training from Organization C, etc. The picture of support functions is complex, because support organizations divide themselves by sectors, gender, or stages of development, and some functions overlap, as exemplified by the long list of major support organizations in St. Louis featured in Table 5.1. The heterogeneity of support organizations between different cities makes this picture even more complex. However, one implication is clear: Since the ways that entrepreneurs solve problems are heterogeneous, and no single right formula exists, no single person can supervise the whole process, and no single organization can provide the right solution or comprehensive services, either. Under such conditions, entrepreneurs try to cultivate a variety of resources in the region.

Co-ordination between ESOs
The availability of various resources within a region, as well as the search and use of these by entrepreneurs, does not mean a complete free-market system in which each support organization exists separately and each entrepreneur atomically selected what he or she needed for the company. When entrepreneurs received a set of support services, they became available often through intentional and functional connections between support organizations.

One entrepreneur described a seamless timing of finance; his business was funded through Arch Grants, Capital Innovators, and a private investor, and the co-ordination between multiple supporters was essential (IT Firm E). The same entrepreneur described that his connections to these support organizations opened further networks, and the company was able to hire two students from Washington University in St. Louis, whose Skandalaris Center had experience in matching students and local startups.

Some co-ordination was the fruit of periodic and scheduled meetings by directors of several support organizations. More formally, some directors served as board members of other organizations. Other less formal co-ordination took place as those directors in the region attended the same entrepreneurial events or spoke as panelists. The case of St. Louis demonstrated that directors of support organizations exchanged highly detailed information about the operations of their organizations, as well as specific companies.

These conversations helped to avoid unnecessary and unintentional overlaps in support.

Both Kansas City and St. Louis enjoyed a good level of co-ordination between support organizations, but that was not always the case. A director of a support organization whose mission was to facilitate co-ordination between ESOs described the previous situation in Kansas City. What she found in the early 2000s was that there were close to 200 entrepreneurship courses offered in the area, which was more than needed. She organized a meeting to gather directors from a couple of dozen organizations and a few key funders. Many directors described how entrepreneurs told them that they did not know how to start companies and needed a crash course. Once those directors and funders realized the excess and overlap, most ESOs rechanneled their resources to other functions (Meyers, interview, March 28, 2014). Thus, just as entrepreneurs living in the same city did not necessarily indicate connectivity between them, support organizations operating in the same city did not indicate co-ordination among them. Support organizations should coordinate intentionally and strategically.

7.3   COMPARISON WITH CURRENT PRACTICE AND POLICY

These findings about entrepreneurship and regional support systems make a sharp contrast to the currently dominant practice and policy. First, there is an extremely blurry distinction in current policy between innovation and entrepreneurship, and an assumption that what is good innovation is also good for entrepreneurship, as discussed in Chapters 1 and 2. Even more broadly, the current policy assumes that invention (scientific discovery), innovation (commercialization of something new), and entrepreneurship (starting a new company and scaling up successfully) can be streamlined in a whole set of activities.

Second, the current policy follows the so-called linear model of development, which assumes "an orderly process, starting with the discovery of new knowledge, moving through various stages of development, and eventually emerging in a final viable form" (Kline 1985, 36). Other scholars have described the assumed processes of the linear model as shown in Table 7.1.

Table 7.1   Major stages in the linear model of development

Furnas (1948)	Kline and Rosenberg (2009)	Godin (2006)
Exploratory research	Research	Basic research
Applied research	Development	Applied research
Development	Production	Development
Production	Marketing	
Sales		

There have been serious scholarly debates about definitions of this linear model, its origins, critiques, and defenses (Nightingale 1998; Edgerton 2004; Hounshell 2004; Godin 2006, 2017; Kline and Rosenberg 2009; Balconi et al. 2010). The reader will be spared the details here, but the point is that the linear model, whatever its simplified or controversial form, has a set of commonalities and enormous influence on practice and policy. We review these influences at the university level and the government level.

The Linear Model in Technology Commercialization Offices by Universities

Most major research universities adapted this linear model for the operation of their technology commercialization offices. We start by describing the stages of technology commercialization at University of Maryland and Ohio State University (Table 7.2), and then extend our analysis to other universities.

While there are some minor differences in technical terminology, it is evident that these two technology transfer offices of major research universities, the University of Maryland and Ohio State, pursue essentially the same strategy based on the linear model: The whole process initiates with research and its scientific discovery or invention. The invention will be protected with intellectual property mechanisms, such as patents or copyrights. Marketing (a general analysis of the size and segments of a market), new products, or revenue generation come in later stages of this development.

These practices at Maryland and Ohio State are not uncommon, but rather typical of major research universities. Indeed, it is the model described by Joe Anderson in Chapter 1. The Association for

*Table 7.2   Major stages of technology commercialization by
University of Maryland and Ohio State*

University of Maryland (2010)	Ohio State University (2018)
Research & development	Pipeline: Research to invention
Invention, disclosure	Evaluation: Technical & patentability
Technology assessment	Protection: Patent application
Patent application, IP protection	Marketing: Technology to industry
Marketing, business proposal	Deal making: License deal to company
Technology commercialization	
New products & services	
Revenue	

University Technology Managers (AUTM), a consortium of university technology offices, has been promoting this model of technology commercialization for years by publishing data related to these stages of development and introducing so-called best practices and case studies. They define the life cycle of technology transfer just as these two universities did: R&D, invention, evaluation, IP protection, marketing, licensing, product development, and public use and economic growth (AUTM 2016a). Their annual survey primarily tracks data about the number of inventions, patents issued, licensing to companies, license revenue, startups coming out of universities, and employment related to those startups (AUTM 2004, 2012, 2016b).[2]

The role of the technology transfer office is to navigate faculty members (and possibly postdoctoral researchers) through the whole process: assessing patentability and assisting in filing patents, providing marketing analysis, and providing small seed grants.

The Linear Model in Government Support

Support systems based on the linear model are also present at the federal and state government levels. The Economic Development Administration (EDA), under the Department of Commerce, is one of the two major agencies to support entrepreneurship activities, along with the Small Business Administration. Their flagship

---

[2]   Other data that AUTM tracks in a special report include gross industrial output and GDP, with multiplier methods (AUTM 2017).

program, the Regional Innovation Strategies (RIS) program, distributes about $15 million annually in two areas: seed fund support investments on the scale of about $150,000 toward organizations that provide seed funds to companies, and i6 Challenge investments on the scale of close to $500,000 to incubators, accelerators, regional funds, and other support organizations. More than half of these recipients are programs or technology transfer offices within universities (EDA 2014, 2015, 2016, 2017). Thus, the practice supported here is essentially the same linear model followed by universities' technology transfer offices but magnified to a larger scale by the federal agencies.

The support system based on the linear model is observed in other branches of the federal government. Block and Keller (2010) described the pervasiveness of state intervention in research and innovation programs in the Defense Advanced Research Projects Agency (DARPA), National Institute of Standards and Technology (NIST), Sandia National Laboratories, and biotechnology areas, and called it the "hidden industrial policy." McCray (2005) and Motoyama et al. (2011) reported that the National Nanotechnology Initiative was established in 2000 to ensure national competitiveness in both science and industry by committing $2 billion in expenditures per annum. However, the disbursement had been almost exclusively to academic research institutions for basic research. The fundamental rationale behind this integration of science and technology policy and industrial policy is the mission of government to support companies as they bridge the so-called "valley of death" between scientific discovery and commercialization (Auerswald and Branscomb 2003). In other words, the government needs to sustain a long process of commercialization activities that could take up to ten years, while the private sector, including banks and venture capitals, aims to fund in a horizon of only three to five years (McNeil et al. 2007). In short, the role of government under the linear model can be summarized as funding science projects (Bhide 2008), and providing venture capital finance and incubator space (Bruneel et al. 2012; Brown and Mason 2017; Brown et al. 2017).

The Gap

These standard support practices to provide scientific research funds, startup seed money, and incubator space have faced increasing criticism for their ineffectiveness. Scholars have so far attributed this ineffectiveness to several factors, such as the insignificant size of investment and bias towards high-tech firms (Grilli and Murtinu 2014; Nightingale et al. 2009), the politicized nature of the selection process (Lerner 2002, 2009), or the inability to bridge to larger, follow-up investments or the lack of comprehensive support (Mason 2015). Harrison and Leitch (2010) have observed that university-based startups started small and remained small. Amezcua (2010) and Amezcua et al. (2013) found that incubator-hosted firms survived better during the incubated period, but were less likely to survive than non-incubated firms after the incubated period. While these critiques are valid, we find that each analysis focused on a rather technical and operational dimension of funding or incubator programs. Here, we propose an alternative explanation. *The currently dominant practice of funding and incubating, essentially pursuing the linear and innovation model, is ineffective because it does not fit the reality of*

Table 7.3   Summary of innovation and entrepreneurship models

	Innovation Model	Entrepreneurship Model
Market	Scientific novelty creates market. Market size will be assessed later.	Entrepreneur creates or finds market. Niche market is small, but with specific customers.
Business plan and competitiveness	Make a good business plan and execute it. Competitiveness will be protected with intellectual property.	Some business plan is needed, but it will evolve. Competitiveness will shift and be added.
Survival of firm	A firm's life should be extended until the market picks up.	A firm should be discontinued if not supported by the market. An entrepreneur can start the next journey.
Finance and growth	Government provides seed money. VC enables massive scale-up.	Bootstrapping and organic growth. Incremental and gradual scale-up.
Support system	A full set of support functions will complete development.	Entrepreneurs keep finding solutions through a variety of support groups.

entrepreneurship and its development process. Table 7.3 summarizes the gap between the innovation and entrepreneurship models.

The differences between the linear innovation model and the entrepreneurship model are clear from the beginning: The linear model presumes that scientific or engineering novelty from cutting-edge technology creates a new market. Typically, people draw the examples of the commercialization of the internet, GPS, high-performance batteries, clean technologies, and the human genome project (Fuchs 2011; Eisler 2012; Rodrik 2014; Greenstein 2015). However, these citations are uncritical (Lester 2008). Not all internet firms came out of technologies based out of universities. Detailed examination reveals that even frequently cited examples, such as Google, Yahoo, and Cisco Systems, did not evolve from the university technology office, or the technology or business idea came from a university professor (see, for example, Levy 2011).

The entrepreneurship model is based on our observation that it is always entrepreneurs who create or find niche markets, which may be small yet have specific customers. In other words, entrepreneurship must be a concrete act with revenue generation. It may be possible to envision a billion-dollar market size in the internet sector or using DNA technologies, but it means nothing if one specific cutting-edge technology does not find a single buyer of a product or service.

The innovation model also emphasizes a business plan and assumes that its sophistication determines the success of the business. Moreover, a highly sophisticated one, judged by some qualified evaluators in a business plan competition, warrants an initial investment either by angel investors, VCs, or the public sector. In addition, the model assumes that, once the business plan is made, the most important element is executing it. Entrepreneurs are the people who execute this plan, perhaps in collaboration with the scientists or engineers who came up with the original cutting-edge technology and business plan. Here, the innovation model assumes that the competitiveness of the business can be protected with intellectual property mechanisms, such as patents, which further reinforces the fixing and execution of a business plan, as well as protecting intellectual property.

On the other hand, the entrepreneurship model assumes that some form of business plan is needed, but it always changes, or rather it should change, based on what entrepreneurs learn, feedback from others, and changes in the market. While there may be impossibly "bad" business plans, the sophistication of a "good" business plan does not determine the success of a business. What entrepreneurs have to prepare for is learning and adaptation, and an execution of a premade plan is not important. One or a few cutting-edge technologies with patent protection does not mean anything because entrepreneurs have to keep adding or changing technologies for clients or markets.

The innovation model further assumes that a "good" startup firm, with protected competitiveness and a sophisticated business plan, must survive through the proof-of-concept and development phases until the product or services come to the market. Hence, the role of the public sector is to provide seed money and an incubator to operate at free or discounted rates to survive this period. The length of this period is unspecified, but many public incubators provide space for three years or longer (Amezcua 2010).

Such survival and dependence on seed money does not apply to the entrepreneurship model. A small amount of seed money, such as $50,000 from the Arch Grants of St. Louis, may be provided, but its purpose is to celebrate entrepreneurship and its importance for the economy and to create a cohort of entrepreneurs, not to enable survival (Motoyama and Knowlton 2016). In fact, a large amount of seed money provides the wrong signal to entrepreneurs by ignoring the need for pivots and feedback from others and by letting them simply execute the formulated business plan. Under the entrepreneurship model, a firm that does not capture market should be discontinued due to the market's harsh nature, and those entrepreneurs can try their next idea instead of prolonging a zombie company. An angel or VC investment may help, but there are other forms of business development and finance, such as bootstrapping and starting small with self-savings. Growing incrementally is powerful, as long as you have customers and cultivate more of them.

Finally, the innovation model assumes that heavy support services will elevate companies to the next level. An incubator or other public agency aims to provide such comprehensive services. However, reality contradicts this. According to the National Business Incubators Association (NBIA 2011), there are more than 1,400 incubators nationwide, but an average incubator is staffed with 1.8 persons and serves 25 client firms. Hannon (2003) described how incubator managers have to function, among other things, as business trainers, free legal advisers, computer experts, social workers, housekeepers, ambassadors to all, and founts of all knowledge. A comprehensive support in theory is practiced by a few staff who have a little expertise on many dimensions.

On the other hand, under the entrepreneurship model, entrepreneurs will go through a variety of support groups because there is no single solution to entrepreneurship, no single organization can provide all kinds of support, and entrepreneurs have to keep learning and evolving.

Caveats and Analogy

While the innovation and entrepreneurship models are largely incompatible, we do not intend to provide a simplistic, black-and-white picture of the world. The reality is mixed, and there are indeed some forms of entrepreneurship, companies, and industries that the innovation model may fit better. Most visibly, a pharmaceutical company can fit the innovation model perfectly. The company and its market will be enabled by a cutting-edge technology, a drug newly invented with a university's technologies. Its competitiveness will be and should be protected by patents to fend off free-riders (companies that do not invest in this research but try to copy the drug formula). The initial seed money is essential, because the company has to survive the first few years when it submits the drug to lengthy lab experiments with animal and human testing, as well as approval by the Federal Drug Administration (FDA), which can easily take one to two years. The product is relatively simple, a drug, the market is specified, people with a specific disease, and the business plan will be relatively straightforward.

However, we have to keep in mind that this case may be significantly in the minority. Our survey in Chapter 4 demonstrated that only 1.9–3.8 percent of companies in Kansas City used patents or licenses from regional universities, while more than 90 percent of firms pursued different forms of entrepreneurship. We conducted interviews with 32 *Inc.* company executives, 46 Arch Grants recipients, and 16 entrepreneurs participating in 1MC, and found only one case (Health Company A) that used university-based cutting-edge technology for a drug-testing device. While interviews and surveys may have a selection bias and may not be the appropriate method to identify a proportion of cases against the total, those findings matched with the regression results in Chapter 3, in which none of the startup or high growth rates correlated with government research funding, university research funding, VC investment, or patents. Nonetheless, if the dominant support policy and practice is appropriate for a minority of cases, we are focusing on the wrong model. We may not need to abandon public support for companies that fit the innovation model, but we must seriously reconsider where the majority of resources should be allocated.

In addition to this issue of disproportion, supporters of the currently dominant practice often rely on a question, how can we create the next Google? Or how can my city or state foster the next Facebook? This rhetoric sets a clear and fancy goal, but this may be the wrong target, because it aims at the top of the top.

To explain why this is the wrong target, we would like to use an analogy about how to create Michael Jordan, the legendary basketball player, by assessing how quantitatively special Michael Jordan is. First, Michael Jordan is 6ft 6in tall, which is the 99.846 percentile in adult males (or 0.154 percent as a probability) (Tall.life 2018). Next, we need to look for someone who can jump extremely high, 48in (0.1 percent of the population according to Topendsports. com 2018). Third, it must be someone with long-range shooting in a, 10–14ft area, the top 1 percentile (Nylon Schooter 2014). Fourth, we need someone with agility in the top 1 percentile. Michael Jordan no doubt has more special talents, but we have already added enough factors to the formula. The probability of finding the next Michael Jordan is:

0.154% (for height) $\times$ 0.1% (jump) $\times$ 1% (long range) $\times$ 1% (agility) = 1.54×10^{-9}

With a U.S. population of 324 million, of which 119 million are adult men, this calculation produces 0.183 person, which means no such person exists in that country. Now imagine that every VC and state government is looking for this next superstar, trying to claim that they have found him, and that investing in him now is the solution. It is simply impossible, yet that is the state of current practice.

Instead, we should consider that entrepreneurship is more like the tip of an iceberg. With the harsh reality of entrepreneurship and its failure rates, less than half of companies survive longer than five years. Of those surviving companies, only a handful companies will achieve high growth, and even a smaller number of them will achieve hyper growth. The Business Dynamics Statistics suggest that only 1.26 percent of firms after five years generate 50 or more employees, and 0.44 percent of them generate 100 or more employees (Census Bureau 2018). Put another way, without surviving companies, there are no high-growth companies. And without high-growth companies, you will have no hyper growth companies. The tip of an iceberg, though it may look like an easy target, is supported by the 90 percent of the iceberg under water. If your city or state wants to have a large tip of an iceberg, you must build the whole and larger iceberg, which includes the invisible bottom.

7.4   POLICY RECOMMENDATIONS

Based on our findings with the entrepreneurship model, we provide the following policy recommendations.

Three Dos

Increase the connectivity within a region.   Since the learning by entrepreneurs is the most essential ingredient for entrepreneurial development, and the learning comes from interacting with other people and organizations, it is crucial for every region to increase connectivity. The case of the Arch Grants recipients, for example, demonstrated that connectivity took place at multiple levels: 1) between entrepreneurs and other entrepreneurs, 2) between entrepreneurs and support organizations, and 3) between support organizations.

It is important for entrepreneurship supporters, organizations, and the public sector to increase these three levels of connectivity within a region. We should also keep in mind that the connectivity here is not necessarily that between aggregated actors, such as industries, universities, and government, but the ones specifically between individuals. The key criterion should be: Does this event or program promote interactions among and learning by targeted entrepreneurs?

Embed connectivity in an entrepreneurial context.   This connectivity for entrepreneurship is not established by simple meeting and networking events, but functions better within an entrepreneurial context. 1MC was the best example, discussing each presenter's business and challenges, and structuring interactions between the presenter and the audience with lengthy Q&A sessions. The format of events critically affects the interactions, because it is natural for entrepreneurship events to end up with self-promotion. Entrepreneurs tend to speak only of the positive sides of their businesses, and support organizations tend to advertise their own programs and activities. Instead, organizers of events and programs should keep in mind that self-promotion and boosterism are not the objective as with a pitch to investors. Rather, the interactions and learning of entrepreneurs are the goal.

Create a go-to place for entrepreneurs. While connectivity is important, the most difficult and crucial step for entrepreneurs is the very beginning: finding the first local resource. Without the first step, there are no further steps. Budding entrepreneurs do not necessarily start with a local chamber of commerce, which is a membership-based organization primarily for established companies, or a local branch of SBA. The door to this go-to place should be open to anyone who is interested in entrepreneurship, including wannabe entrepreneurs. It may include people other than entrepreneurs, such as programmers, web designers, engineers, marketing specialists, operation specialists, and so on. Such a go-to place can be an organization as well. In Kansas City, SourceLink functions as a referral service to introduce other organizations and services to entrepreneurs. It could be a regular event with a predicted schedule; for example, 1MC takes place every Wednesday. Similarly, ITEN in St. Louis hosts on the second Thursday of every month at a local restaurant.

While inclusiveness is the key, a go-to network may attract certain kinds of entrepreneurs; for example, the majority of 1MC participants are Caucasian male in the IT sector. We observed that entrepreneurs in other sectors still attended 1MC meetings because they liked the interactions and vibe. Later, some of them branched out and created similar networking events, such as Educators as Entrepreneurs since February 2014, North Kansas City since 2014, and GuildIt for entrepreneurs in the creative sector since May 2015. The tendency for homogeneity and difficulty of inclusiveness are important issues, and much more research is needed. However, since the first step is the toughest, it is better to have some form of go-to place than no such place. As the network and participants grow, entrepreneurs sort out and spin off their networks as well.

Two Don'ts

Avoid the standard practice of public venture funds and incubators. As discussed earlier, the most common form of entrepreneurship support by the public sector is sponsorship through new venture funds and incubators (Lerner 2002; Amezcua et al. 2013). This is a natural response, because if you ask entrepreneurs the most pressing problem, the answer is most likely the lack of money. However, providing money does not necessarily get rid of problems or make entrepreneurs succeed. Ewing Marion Kauffman, Kansas City's billionaire entrepreneur, emphasized: "All of the money in the world cannot solve problems unless we work together. And if we work together, there is no problem in the world that can stop us, as we seek to develop people to their highest potential." To reach the highest potential, every entrepreneur has to learn, and an artificial lift from venture funds does not make it closer.

At the same time, we do not intend to deny the entire existence of such standard practice, and one can follow standard practice with caveats. Realistically, there are many public venture funds and incubators already operating in the U.S. and other parts of the world, and those public programs cannot be terminated politically. It may be easier to consider how to re-tailor their operations.

Taking the central finding of this book, the importance of the interactions and learning of entrepreneurs, public venture funds and incubators can be used to promote entrepreneurship if they can embed the interaction and learning element in their operations. Once again, the purpose of the Arch Grants was not to inject a large sum of money, but to celebrate entrepreneurship regionwide and to create a cohort of entrepreneurs. An incubator need not be a place to provide free or cheap office space, in which busy and hardworking entrepreneurs come to the office in the morning and go home at night, but could instead be a place where entrepreneurs gather and interact. There can be creative ways to do so by providing co-working spaces, instituting interactive programs, and co-locating key support service organizations. While more research is needed about how to implement this idea, there are emerging examples such as Cambridge Innovation Center (CIC) in Boston and St. Louis, T-REX in St. Louis, and 1871 in Chicago.

Do not aim to captivate entrepreneurs or provide full services. We need to keep in mind that a go-to place for entrepreneurs or incubators should not be a strategy for any support organization to attract new entrepreneurs, nor a one-stop and final-stop shop. Since entrepreneurs need to cultivate a variety of sources, and no organization can provide comprehensive support, this go-to place should be only a beginning point, where curious entrepreneurs can find their next resources. No single person or organization can provide all the answers for entrepreneurial journeys. Instead, any support organization should function as a hub of referrals for further resources. In order to do so, every support organization needs to be connected to other support organizations.

7.5 FURTHER IMPLICATIONS

Entrepreneurship and the Just-in-Time Production System?

Our comparison of the innovation and entrepreneurship models was at the tactical level and process oriented. There are broader theoretical differences between the two models. At the fundamental level, the philosophy of the innovation model is rationalistic. First, you assume that the answer or single path for entrepreneurship exists, and then you can identify a common set of hurdles faced by entrepreneurs. It also assumes that the identified market and proposed business plan are right, and that is why executing the business plan is the priority. Then, funding for survival and comprehensive support are justified.

In contrast, the fundamental philosophy of the entrepreneurship model is pragmatic, where we assume no right answer. Since entrepreneurship is heterogeneous, challenges for entrepreneurs are different. Thus, no prescription exists, and entrepreneurs will only encounter challenges and solutions through experimentation. Then, entrepreneurs have to learn from others and keep tapping different peers and support organizations. Connectivity between entrepreneurs and support organizations is essential. In sum, the support system requires adjustment over time and not adherence to a predetermined goal or path.

These philosophical and theoretical differences parallel the differences between Taylorism and the just-in-time production system. Under Taylorism, an engineer identifies and designs what is supposed to be the most efficient production system (Taylor 1903). The task for the rest of the factory workers is to execute this system, and efficiency is achieved as long as those workers do not deviate from the designed system. As Taylor himself recognized in titling his book *The Principles of Scientific Management* (1911), this approach is highly scientific and rationalistic. A separate marketing analysis will forecast the market demand, which determines the scale of production and investment.

In contrast, under the just-in-time system, most notably developed by Toyota, factory workers start with an assumption that every production system has problems, and only their continuous improvement, based on experiments and learning, can make it better (Fujimoto 1999; Hino 2002; Liker 2004). The scale of production is determined based on market demand, that is, when consumers order the car, not by a sophisticated marketing prediction. This system is pragmatic and experiment oriented. The superiority of the latter production system has been well documented since all the major U.S. automobile manufacturers lost market share to their Japanese counterparts starting in the 1980s, which led to efforts by the Big Three to emulate just-in-time manufacturing.

The innovation model can be seen as a reflection of scientific and rationalistic Taylorism, in which scientific novelty creates the market, the business plan lays out the market demand and pathways for the firm's development, and the entrepreneur's major task is the execution of the business plan. On the other hand, the entrepreneurship model closely resembles the just-in-time system, in which entrepreneurs have to figure out and revise their business plans based on signals from the market and feedback from peers, mentors, and other supporters. Experiments, learning, and continuous improvement are the key, instead of the single right answer for entrepreneurship.

From Technology Transfer to Human Transfer

Earlier, we described the efforts by technology transfer offices to track data on university spin-offs, patents, and licenses. In addition to its use in the innovation model, we need to revisit the meaning of this tracked data. In 2016, AUTM reported that its member institutions generated 1,024 startups, a number that has been increasing over the last few years and might sound impressive. However, we have to put this number in context. This number came out of responses by 169 universities and research institutions. Thus, each university created 6.06 firms on average. In the meantime, these 169 institutions spent $66.9 billion in research, so that would mean every $65 million spent on research leads to a new company, which is not so impressive. Unfortunately, AUTM does not track the number of people employed by university-based startups, while we know that, anecdotally, university spin-offs are usually very small and stay small, rarely over ten employees (Harrison and Leitch 2010). Similarly, the member institutions received $2.963 billion in revenue for licensing, which means the return rate for one research dollar is 4.4 cents. To date, there has not been any academic or public discussion about what these numbers mean or what amount is acceptable as public investment. We ought to start a debate about the significance of these numbers, particularly given that many research universities are public institutions, and even private universities receive billions of research dollars from the federal government.

At the same time, we have observed that universities can play different roles in entrepreneurship. Based on the principle of entrepreneurship, universities can increase the connectivity of entrepreneurs within the region. Rather than technology transfer through patents or licenses, perhaps there can be human transfer of students to local startup firms, as one example. University courses may not prepare students to run businesses, but universities can inspire students toward entrepreneurship. Again, the objective of a student business plan competition should not be to win large amounts of resources but to attract and inspire students. Furthermore, by inviting local entrepreneurs to be the judges of the competition, universities can establish visible connections between students and entrepreneurs. There may be other ways to increase this connectivity through internship programs, though universities must make sure that, to avoid exploiting students, companies and students make solid agreements about business ideas and technology uses.

Data for Entrepreneurship

Based on these philosophical and tactical differences between the models, we propose to revisit the linear model of innovation, which is pervasive in science and technology policy, technology commercialization, and economic development policy. Most of the funding for scientific knowledge and support services to get through the "valley of death" does not yield fruit in entrepreneurship, even when bridging efforts of technology commercialization are present, because this approach prioritizes neither market demand nor experiential learning of entrepreneurs. In other words, the linear model largely does not reflect the reality of entrepreneurship. However, the linear model may apply to a small fraction of capital-intensive sectors like pharmaceuticals, as mentioned earlier. Nonetheless, we need to be conscious about the objective and priority of public policies.

The influence of the linear model is also evident in policies to measure innovation and entrepreneurship. Since Congress mandated that the National Science Board, the governing body of the National Science Foundation, publish *Science and Engineering Indicators* in 1973, this report has become an authoritative index of the state of science and engineering productivity in this country (Grupp and Mogee 2004). Chapter 8 of this annual report specifically tracks inventions, knowledge transfer, and innovation, as measured by peer-reviewed publications; patents, including those owned by universities; license revenue to universities; business startups created by technology transfer offices; and VC investment (NSF 2018). These are not neutral indicators that will harmlessly help science and policy decisions, but normative ones that set the tone for deciding outputs, outcomes, goals, and even which processes of innovation to emphasize (Godin 2017). However, Chapter 3 of this book demonstrated that many of these indicators have no correlation to entrepreneurship activities. Thus, we are aiming for the wrong targets.

At minimum, we should acknowledge that science and technology activities and entrepreneurship activities are different. Science-based development is not necessarily the twenty-first-century model, and increasing peer-review publications, patents, and research expenditures do not lead to more entrepreneurship. In other words, an increased budget for scientific research should not be naively applied to industrial or economic policy, as we witnessed in the National Nanotechnology Initiative (Motoyama et al. 2011).

Having said this, it is difficult to propose a set of countermeasures. The primary sources of entrepreneurship development, connectivity and learning, are process activities, not output-oriented indicators like patents or amount of investment. The number of mentors on a list does not mean anything unless we can demonstrate that entrepreneurs are connected and learning from those mentors. Moreover, since much of the learning takes place at the local level, tracing data at the national level likely obscures the dynamics of entrepreneurship. At least, data should be collected from the local level and later aggregated to the national level.

While we do not have a complete prescription for which data to track for entrepreneurship, we have presented several hints throughout this book. Interviews can best portray the nature and level of learning by entrepreneurs, though as a data-collection method it is the most time intensive and hardest to achieve scale. Surveys can expand the scale considerably, as long as you can preidentify specific mentors, organizations, or sources for learning, a process that is possible for support organizations but highly complicated for individual supporters. Analysis of social media, like Twitter, can expand the scale substantially, while at the same time making it less effective to demonstrate the nature of connections and learning. However, the Twitter accounts we analyzed in Chapter 6 are only an initial example from social media. In the future, content analysis or uses of other social media can enrich the dimensions about connectivity and learning.

The primary objective of this book is to shed light on the fundamentals of entrepreneurship and support mechanisms that have been overlooked in the shadow of the linear and innovation model. We believe that we have uncovered those fundamentals of the entrepreneurship model from the two regional cases and national level analysis with multiple sets of data and methods. Still, our findings become a basis for new questions. How does the local system for entrepreneurship evolve over time? If a newly emerging entrepreneurship community attracts a specific demographic, such as the white male in the IT sector as 1MC tended to do, and different segments of entrepreneurs branch out, such as one for education services and another one for artist entrepreneurs, what does the structure and map of different kinds of entrepreneurs within a region look like? What separates the groups and prevents them from interacting?

We laid out principles of public-sector engagement to foster entrepreneurship development, but these principles may not be comprehensive in scope, and there can be many tactical issues about program development and interorganizational co-ordination. As the field of entrepreneurship continues to grow in recent years, we need to persist in tackling these next important questions theoretically and practically.

APPENDIX

Table A.1   Highest and lowest 15 of the dependent variables in Chapter 2

Highest 15	All Industry		High-Tech Sectors		High-Growth Firms	
		Ratio		Ratio		Ratio
	Provo-Orem, UT	0.2123	Boulder, CO	50.6	Boulder, CO	13.7
	Palm Coast, FL	0.2115	Washington, DC-VA-MD-WV	25.7	Washington DC-VA-MD-WV	12.9
	Las Vegas-Paradise, NV	0.2016	San Jose-Sunnyvale, CA	22.1	Provo-Orem, UT	10.7
	Miami-Fort Lauderdale, FL	0.1999	Fort Collins-Loveland, CO	21.8	Huntsville, AL	10.3
	Orlando-Kissimmee, FL	0.1806	Cheyenne, WY	21.0	Austin-San Marcos, TX	10.1
	Cape Coral-Fort Myers, FL	0.1805	Denver-Aurora, CO	20.3	San Francisco-Oakland, CA	7.8
	Austin-San Marcos, TX	0.1773	Salt Lake City, UT	20.1	Raleigh-Cary, NC	7.0
	McAllen-Edinburg, TX	0.1747	San Francisco-Oakland, CA	19.8	San Jose-Santa Clara, CA	7.0
	Tampa-St. Petersburg, FL	0.1681	Colorado Springs, CO	19.7	Boston-Cambridge, MA-NH	6.9
	Phoenix-Mesa, AZ	0.1672	Bend, OR	19.1	Trenton-Ewing, NJ	6.8
	Naples-Marco Island, FL	0.1659	Seattle-Tacoma, WA	18.8	Atlanta-Marietta, GA	6.6
	Dallas-Fort Worth, TX	0.1650	Provo-Orem, UT	18.1	Denver-Aurora, CO	6.6
	Sarasota-North Port, FL	0.1629	Corvallis, OR	17.3	Logan, UT-ID	6.3
	Atlanta-Marietta, GA	0.1622	Raleigh-Cary, NC	17.0	Salt Lake City, UT	6.2
	Houston-Baytown, TX	0.1622	Huntsville, AL	17.0	Bridgeport-Stamford, CT	6.2

Lowest 15	Ratio		Ratio	
Oshkosh-Neenah, WI	0.0798	Pine Bluff, AR	1.7	106 MSAs have no high-growth firms
Saginaw, MI	0.0785	El Centro, CA	1.6	
Fond du Lac, WI	0.0775	Sumter, SC	1.6	
Michigan City-La Porte, IN	0.0771	Rocky Mount, NC	1.6	
Muncie, IN	0.0768	Madera-Chowchilla, CA	1.5	
Altoona, PA	0.0763	Victoria, TX	1.4	
Decatur, IL	0.0750	St. Joseph, MO-KS	1.1	
Steubenville, OH-WV	0.0750	Jonesboro, AR	1.1	
El Paso, TX	0.0750	Lewiston, ID-WA	1.1	
Spokane, WA	0.0736	Merced, CA	1.1	
Mansfield, OH	0.0727	Goldsboro, NC	0.7	
Danville, IL	0.0722	Steubenville, OH-WV	0.7	
Lima, OH	0.0700	Fond du Lac, WI	0.7	
Johnstown, PA	0.0679	Wheeling, WV-OH	0.6	
Wheeling, WV-OH	0.0657	Elmira, NY	0.5	

Table A.2   Descriptive statistics of regression variables

	Min	1st Qtr	Median	Mean	3rd Qtr	Max
BDS all-industry startup	0.0657	0.0957	0.1101	0.1133	0.1252	0.2123
NETS high-tech startup	0.5277	3.1876	4.9171	6.3343	8.1045	50.6160
Inc. high-growth	0.2251	3.9350	6.7391	9.0194	10.2517	57.0142
Population in 2011	55,439	143,777	253,997	713,398	560,372	19,015,900
Pop growth 2006–10	–0.0364	0.0169	0.0368	0.0400	0.0609	0.1588
Ave. household income	63,260	83,910	92,591	95,969	102,771	200,020
Population flux	0.0278	0.0601	0.0730	0.0823	0.0937	0.2532
Econ. diversity	1.0000	1.0000	2.0000	1.9730	2.0000	6.0000
LQ of high-tech	0.2000	0.5000	0.7000	0.7790	0.9000	4.6000
Patents / 100K	0.3900	5.6900	12.0100	25.3200	26.5000	503.3600
Research I	0.0000	0.0000	0.0000	0.2814	0.0000	7.0000
SBIR / cap	0.0000	0.0000	0.9061	6.8764	5.2131	145.9100
NIH / cap	0.0000	0.0000	3.2350	77.1320	87.1620	1955.1100
VC investment	0	0	0	395,179	20,978	78,770,707
College completion	10.2000	20.4900	26.1400	27.2600	32.4100	60.7400
High school completion	76.2400	91.9400	93.7700	93.2800	95.2900	100.0000

Interview List

Aulet, Bill. Managing Director, Martin Center for Entrepreneurship. Massachusetts Institute of Technology. November 19, 2013. Kansas City, MO.

Brasunas, Jim. Executive Director. ITEN. December 10, 2012. August 1, 2013. February 13, 2014. St. Louis, MO.

Burke, Ben. Director of Entrepreneurship. Arch Grants. November 24, 2014. St. Louis, MO.

Chmelir, Francis. Director of Operations. ITEN. August 1, 2013. St. Louis, MO.

Cobb, Joni. President of Pipeline. January 17, 2014; April 22, 2014. Kansas City, MO.

Duttia, Suren. Advisor to Washington University in St. Louis. August 24, 2012. St. Louis, MO.

Gulve, Eric, Ph.D. President. BioGenerator. October 1, 2013. St. Louis, MO.

Hagan, Patty. September 11, 2014 and October 1, 2014.

Harrington, Ken. Managing Director. Skandalaris Center for Entrepreneurship. Washington University in St. Louis. December 10, 2012. St Louis, MO; June 22, 2015, Kansas City, MO.

Helzberg, Bernett. Chairman of Helzberg Entrepreneurship Mentorship Program (HEMP) and former CEO of Helzberg Diamond. December 18, 2012. Kansas City, MO.

Hodel, Kate Pope. Special Projects. SourceLink. January 30, 2017. Kansas City, MO.

Imster, Ginger. CEO of Arch Grants. February 13, 2014. St. Louis, MO.

Menietti, Matt. Director of Operations. Capital Innovators. November 15, 2013. St. Louis.

Meyers, Maria. Executive Director. SourceLink. March 28, 2014. January 30, 2017. Kansas City, MO.

Rush, Toby. CEO of EyeVerify. January 24, 2013. Kansas City, MO.

Sheridan, Travis. President. St. Louis Venture Café. December 9, 2013, St. Louis, MO.

References

Acs, Zoltan, Luc Anselin, and Attila Varga. 2002. "Patents and innovation counts as measures of regional production of new knowledge." *Research Policy* 31 (7): 1069–86.

Acs, Zoltan and Catherine Armington. 2003. "Endogenous growth and entrepreneurial activity in cities." Discussion paper CES 03-02. Washington DC: Center for Economic Studies, Census Bureau.

Acs, Zoltan and Catherine Armington. 2006. *Entrepreneurship, Geography, and American Economic Growth.* Cambridge: Cambridge University Press.

Acs, Zoltan and David B. Audretsch. 1990. *Innovation and Small Firms.* Cambridge, MA: MIT Press.

Acs, Zoltan, David B. Audretsch, and Bradley Feld. 1994a. "R&D spillovers and recipient firm size." *Review of Economics and Statistics* 76: 336–40.

Acs, Zoltan, David B. Audretsch, and Maryann P. Feldman. 1994b. "R&D spillovers and innovative activity." *Managerial and Decision Economics* 15: 131–8.

Acs, Zoltan, David Audretsch, and Erik E. Lehmann. 2013. "The knowledge spillover theory of entrepreneurship." *Small Business Economics* 41 (4): 757–74.

Acs, Zoltan, Pontus Braunerhjelm, David B. Audretsch, and Bo Carlsson. 2009. "The knowledge spillover theory of entrepreneurship." *Small Business Economics* 32 (1): 15–30.

Acs, Zoltan and Pamela Mueller. 2008. "Employment effects of business dynamics: Mice, gazelles, and elephants." *Small Business Economics* 30 (1): 85–100.

Acs, Zoltan and David J. Storey. 2004. "Introduction: Entrepreneurship and economic development." *Regional Studies* 38 (8): 781–877.

Allen, Robert Loring. 1991. *Opening Doors: The Life and Work of Joseph Schumpeter.* New Brunswick, NJ: Transaction Publishers.

Almeida, Paul and Bruce Kogut. 1997. "The exploration of technological diversity and the geographic localization of innovation." *Small Business Economics* 9 (1): 21–31.

Amezcua, Alejandro S. 2010. "Boon or boondoggle?: Business incubation as entrepreneurship policy." Syracuse, NY: Syracuse University.

Amezcua, Alehandro S., Matthew G. Grimes, Steven W. Bradley, and Johan Wiklund. 2013. "Organizational sponsorship and founding environments: A contingency view on the survival of business-incubated firms, 1994–2007." *Academy of Management Journal* 56 (6): 1628–54.

Anselin, Luc, Attila Varga, and Zoltan Acs. 1997. "Local geographic spillovers between university research and high technology innovations." *Journal of Urban Economics* 42: 422–48.

Arch Grants. 2014. "Arch Grants data by cohorts." August 26.

Arch Grants. 2015. "About Arch Grants." Accessed May 19, 2005 at http://archgrants.org/about/.

Arenson, Adam. 2011. *The Great Heart of the Republic: St. Louis and the Cultural Civil War*. Cambridge, MA: Harvard University Press.

Asheim, Bjorn T. 1996. "Industrial districts as 'learning regions': A condition for prosperity." *European Planning Studies* 4 (4): 379–400.

Asheim, Bjorn T. and Arne Isaksen. 1997. "Location, agglomeration and innovation: Towards regional innovation systems in Norway?" *European Planning Studies* 5 (3): 299–330.

Audretsch, David B. and Maryann P. Feldman. 1996. "R&D spillovers and the geography of innovation and production." *American Economic Review* 86 (3): 630–40.

Audretsch, David B. and Maryann P. Feldman. 2004. "Knowledge spillovers and the geography of innovation." In J. Vernon Henderson and Jacques-Francois Thisse (eds.), *Handbook of Urban and Regional Economics, 4: Cities and Geography*. Amsterdam: Elsevier, pp. 2713–40.

Audretsch, David B. and Michael Fritsch. 1994. "The geography of firm births in Germany." *Regional Studies* 28 (4): 359–65.

Auerswald, Philip E. and Lewis M. Branscomb. 2003. "Valleys of death and Darwinian seas: Financing the invention to innovation transition in the United States." *Journal of Technology Transfer* 28 (3): 227–39.

Aulet, Bill. 2013. *Disciplined Entrepreneurship: 24 Steps to a Successful Startup*. New York: Wiley.

AUTM. 2004. "AUTM U.S. licensing activity survey." Deerfield, IL: Association of University Technology Managers.

AUTM. 2012. "AUTM U.S. licensing activity survey." Deerfield, IL: Association of University Technology Managers.

AUTM. 2016a. "AUTM U.S. licensing activity survey." Deerfield, IL: Association of University Technology Managers.

AUTM. 2016b. "Infographics." Accessed September 18, 2018 at https://www.autm.net/AUTMMain/media/SurveyReportsPDF/AUTM-FY2016-Infographic-Blank-Lifecycle-WEB.pdf.

AUTM. 2017. "Economic contribution of university/nonprofit inventions in the United States: 1996–2015." Deerfield, IL: Association of University Technology Managers.

Balconi, Margherita, Stefano Brusoni, and Luigi Orsenigo. 2010. "In defense of the linear model: An essay." *Research Policy* 39: 1–13.

Barnes, Harper. 1974. "Kansas City modern." *Atlantic Monthly* (February), 60–67.

BATS. 2016. "About the BATS exchanges." Accessed October 24, 2016 at https://batstrading.com/about/.

Bayless, Pamela. 1978. "What's doing in Kansas City." *New York Times* (December 24), XX7.

Bessen, James and Michael J. Meurer. 2008. *Patent Failure: How Judges, Bureaucrats, and Lawyers Put Innovators at Risk*. Princeton, NJ: Princeton University Press.

Bettencourt, Luis M.A., Jose Lobo, and Deborah Strumsky. 2007. "Invention in the city: Increasing returns to patenting as a scaling function of metropolitan size." *Research Policy* 36: 107–20.

Bhide, Amar. 2008. *Venturesome Economy*. Princeton, NJ: Princeton University Press.

Birch, David L. 1981. "Who creates jobs?" *The Public Interest* 65: 3–14.

Birch, David L. 1987. *Job Creation in America: How Our Smallest Companies Put the Most People to Work*. New York: Free Press.

Block, Fred and Matthew Keller. 2010. *State of Innovation: Technology Policy in the United States*. Boulder, CO: Paradigm.

Bos, Jaap W.B. and Erik Stam. 2013. "Gazelles and industry growth: A study of young high-growth firms in the Netherlands." *Industrial and Corporate Change* 23 (1): 145–69.

Braunerhjelm, Pontus, Zoltan Acs, David B. Audretsch, and Bo Carlsson. 2010. "The missing link: Knowledge diffusion and entrepreneurship in endogenous growth." *Small Business Economics* 34 (2): 105–25.

Breznitz, Dan and Mollie Taylor. 2014. "The communal roots of entre-preneurial-technological growth – social fragmentation and stagnation: Reflection on Atlanta's technology cluster." *Entrepreneurship and Regional Development* 26 (3–4): 375–96.

Brown, Ross and Colin Mason. 2017. "Looking inside the spiky bits: A critical review and conceptualisation of entrepreneurial ecosystems." *Small Business Economics* 49 (1): 11–30.

Brown, Ross and Suzanne Mawson. 2016. "The geography of job creation in high-growth firms: The implications of 'growing abroad.'" *Environment and Planning C: Government and Policy* 34 (2): 207–27.

Brown, Ross, Suzanne Mawson, and Colin Mason. 2017. "Myth-busting and entrepreneurship policy: The case of high-growth firms." *Entrepreneurship and Regional Development* 29 (5–6): 414–43.

Bruneel, Johan, Tiago Ratinho, Bart Clarysse, and Aard Groen. 2012. "Evolution of business incubators: Comparing demand and supply of business incubation services across different incubator generations." *Technovation* 32 (2): 110–21.

Buffalo Billion. 2016. "About the competition." Accessed December 22, 2016 at https://buffalobillion.ny.gov/43north.

Bureau of Labor Statistics. 2017. "Survival of private sector establishments by opening year." Accessed February 17, 2017 at https://www.bls.gov/bdm/us_age_naics_00_table7.txt.

Buss, Terry F. 2001. *Capital, Emerging High-Growth Firms and Public Policy: The Case against Federal Intervention*. Westport, CT: Praeger Publishers.

Carlsson, Bo and Ann-Charlotte Fridh. 2002. "Technology transfer in the United States universities." *Journal of Evolutionary Economics* 12 (1): 199–232.

Carnegie Commission on Higher Education. 2013. "The basic classification." New York: Carnegie Endowment.

Castells, Manuel. 1989. *Informational City: Information Technology, Economic Restructuring, and the Urban-Regional Process*. Oxford: Blackwell.

Census Bureau. 2013. "Overview – business dynamics statistics, footnote 1." Accessed November 12, 2013 at http://www.census.gov/ces/dataproducts/bds/overview.html#footnote1.

Census Bureau. 2014. "American community survey." Accessed May 23, 2016 at https://www.census.gov/acs/www/data/data-tables-and-tools/index.php.

Census Bureau. 2016. "Business dynamics statistics: Firm characteristics data tables." Accessed May 17, 2016 at http://www.census.gov/ces/dataproducts/bds/data_firm.html.

Census Bureau. 2018. "Business dynamics statistics: Firm age by firm size." Accessed September 5, 2018 at https://www.census.gov/ces/dataproducts/bds/data_firm.html.

Chapple, Karen, Ann Markusen, Greg Schrock, Daisaku Yamamoto, and Pingkang Yu. 2004. "Gauging metropolitan 'high-tech' and 'I-tech' activity." *Economic Development Quarterly* 18 (1): 10–29.

Chesbrough, Henry, Wim Vanhaverbeke, and Joel West. 2006. *Open Innovation: Research a New Paradigm.* Oxford: Oxford University Press.

Chinitz, Benjamin. 1961. "Contrasts in agglomeration: New York and Pittsburgh." *American Economic Review* 51 (2): 279–89.

Cohen, Boyd. 2006. "Sustainable valley entrepreneurial ecosystem." *Business Strategy and the Environment* 15 (1): 1–14.

Collins, Jim. 2001. *Good to Great: Why Some Companies Make the Leap and Others Don't.* New York: HarperCollins.

Cooke, Philip. 1992. "Regional innovation systems: Competitive regulation in the new Europe." *Geoforum* 23 (3): 365–82.

Cooke, Philip. 1998. "Introduction: Origins of the concept." In Hans-Joachim Braczyk, Philip Cooke, and Martin Heidenreich (eds.), *Regional Innovation Systems.* London: University College London Press, pp. 2–26.

Cooke, Philip. 2001. "Regional innovation systems, clusters, and the knowledge economy." *Industrial and Corporate Change* 10 (4): 945–74.

Cronon, William. 1991. *Nature's Metropolis: Chicago and the Great West.* New York: W.W. Norton.

Davidsson, Per, Leif Lindmark, and Christer Olofsson. 1994. "New firm formation and regional development in Sweden." *Regional Studies* 28 (4): 395–410.

De la Merced, Michael J. 2008. "InBev to buy Anheuser-Busch for $52 billion." *New York Times* (July 14). Accessed February 4, 2019 at www.nytimes.com/2008/07/14/business/worldbusiness/14iht-14beer.14460585.html.

DeVol, Ross C., Kevin Klowden, Armen Bedroussian, and Benjamin Yeo. 2009. *North America's High-Tech Economy: The Geography of Knowledge-Based Industries.* Santa Monica, CA: Milken Institute.

Doreian, Patrick and Katherine L. Woodard. 1992. "Fixed list versus snowball selection of social networks." *Social Science Research* 21: 216–33.

Drucker, Peter F. 1985 [2015]. *Innovation and Entrepreneurship: Practice and Principles.* New York: Routledge.

Drucker, Joshua and Edward Feser. 2012. "Regional industrial structure and agglomeration economies: An analysis of productivity in three manufacturing industries." *Regional Science and Urban Economics* 42 (1–2): 1–14.

Economist. 2009. "Entrepreneurship." *The Economist*, April 27.

EDA. 2014. "2014 regional innovation strategies program – awardees." Economic Development Administration. Accessed September 19, 2018 at https://www.eda.gov/oie/ris/i6/2014/.

EDA. 2015. "2015 regional innovation strategies program – awardees." Economic Development Administration. Accessed September 19, 2018 at https://www.eda.gov/oie/ris/i6/2015/.

EDA. 2016. "2016 regional innovation strategies program – awardees." Economic Development Administration. Accessed September 19, 2018 at https://www.eda.gov/oie/ris/i6/2016/.

EDA. 2017. "2017 regional innovation strategies program – awardees." Economic Development Administration. Accessed September 19, 2018 at https://www.eda.gov/oie/ris/i6/2017/.

Edgerton, David. 2004. "The 'linear model' did not exist." In Karl Grandin and Nina Wormbs (eds.), *Reflections on the History and Historiography of Science and Research in Industry in the 20th Century.* Sagamore Beach, MA: Science History Publications, pp. 31–57.

Edquist, Charles. 1997. *Systems of Innovation: Technologies, Institutions and Organizations.* London: Painter.

Edquist, Charles. 2005. "Systems of innovation: Perspectives and challenges." In Jan Fagerberg, David C. Mowery, and Richard R. Nelson (eds.), *The Oxford Handbook of Innovation.* Oxford: Oxford University Press, pp. 181–208.

Edquist, Charles, Leif Hommen, and Maureen McKelvey. 2001. *Innovation and Employment: Process versus Product Innovation.* Cheltenham: Edward Elgar Publishing.

Eisler, Matthew N. 2012. *Overpotential: Fuel Cells, Futurism, and the Making of a Power Panacea.* Rutgers University Press.

Etzkowitz, Henry. 2008. *The Triple Helix: University-Industry-Government Innovation in Action.* New York: Routledge.

Etzkowitz, Henry and Loet Leydesdorff. 2000. "The dynamics of innovation: from national systems and 'Mode 2' to a triple helix of university–industry–government relations." *Research Policy* 29: 109–23.

Evans, Alan W. 1986. "Comparisons of agglomeration: Or what Chinitz really said." *Urban Studies* 23 (5): 387–9.

Fairlie, Robert, Arnobio Morelix, E.J. Reedy, and Joshua Russell. 2015. *Kauffman Index of Startup Activity*. Kansas City, MO: Ewing Marion Kauffman Foundation.

FBI. 2013. *Crime in the United States*. Washington DC: Federal Bureau of Investigation.

Feldman, Maryann P. 1999. "The new economics of innovation, spillovers and agglomeration: A review of empirical studies." *Economics of Innovation and New Technology* 8 (1–2): 5–25.

Feldman, Maryann P. 2000. "Location and innovation: The new economic geography of innovation, spillovers and agglomeration." In Gordon L. Clark, Maryann P. Feldman, and Meric S. Gertler (eds.), *Oxford Handbook of Economic Geography*. Oxford: Oxford University Press, pp. 373–94.

Feldman, Maryann. 2001. "The entrepreneurial event revisited: Firm formation in a regional context." *Industrial and Corporate Change* 10: 861–91.

Feldman, Maryann P. 2003. "The locational dynamics of the US biotech industry: Knowledge externalities and the anchor hypothesis." *Industry and Innovation* 10 (3): 311–29.

Feldman, Maryann P. and David B. Audretsch. 1999. "Innovation in cities: Science-based diversity, specialization and localized competition." *European Economic Review* 43: 409–29.

Feldman, Maryann P. and Pierre Desrochers. 2003. "Research universities and local economic development: Lessons from the history of the Johns Hopkins University." *Industry and Innovation* 10 (1): 5–24.

Feldman, Maryann P. and Pierre Desrochers. 2004. "Truth for its own sake: Academic culture and technology transfer at Johns Hopkins University." *Minerva* 42 (2): 105–26.

Feldman, Maryann P. and Richard Florida. 1994. "The geographic sources of innovation: Technological infrastructure and product innovation in the United States." *Annals of the Association of American Geographers* 84 (2): 210–29.

Feser, Edward. 2003. "What regions do rather than make: A proposed set of knowledge-based occupation clusters." *Urban Studies* 40 (10): 1937–58.

Fogarty, Michael S. and Amit K. Sinha. 1999. "Why older regions can't generalize from Route 128 and Silicon Valley: University–industry relationships and regional innovation systems." In Lewis M. Branscomb, Fumio Kodama, and Richard Florida (eds.), *Industrializing Knowledge: University–Industry Linkages in Japan and the United States*. Cambridge, MA: MIT Press, pp. 473–509.

Frank, Mark. 1998. "Schumpeter on entrepreneurs and innovation: A reappraisal." *Journal of the History of Economic Thought* 20 (4): 505–16.

Franke, Nikolaus, Florian Schirg, and Kathrin Reinsberger. 2016. "The frequency of end-user innovation: A re-estimation of extant findings." *Research Policy* 45 (8): 1684–9.

Freeman, Christopher. 1982. *The Economics of Industrial Innovation*, 2nd edn. Cambridge, MA: MIT Press.

Freeman, Christopher. 2002. "Continental, national and sub-national innovation systems: Complementarity and economic growth." *Research Policy* 31 (2): 191–211.

Fritsch, Michael and Pamela Mueller. 2008. "The effect of new business formation on regional development over time: The case of Germany." *Small Business Economics* 30 (1): 15–29.

Fuchs, Victor R. 2011. *Who Shall Live?: Health, Economics and Social Choice*. Singapore: World Scientific.

Fujimoto, Takahiro. 1999. *The Evolution of a Manufacturing System at Toyota*. New York: Oxford University Press.

Furnas, C.C. 1948. *Research in Industry: Its Organization and Management*. New York: D. Van Nostrand Company.

Gassmann, Oliver. 2006. "Opening up the innovation process: Towards an agenda." *R&D Management* 36 (3): 223–8.

Gibson, Campbell. 1998. Population of the 100 largest cities and other urban places in the United States: 1790 to 1990. In *Working Paper 27*. Washington DC: Census Bureau.

Girvan, Michelle and Mark E.J. Newman. 2002. "Community structure in social and biological networks." *Proceedings of the National Academy of Sciences* 99 (2): 7821–6.

Glaeser, Edward L., Hedi D. Kallal, Jose A. Scheinkman, and Andrei Shleifer. 1992. "Growth in cities." *Journal of Political Economy* 100 (6): 1126–52.

Godin, Benoît. 2003. "The emergence of S&T indicators: Why did governments supplement statistics with indicators?" *Research Policy* 32 (4): 679–91.

Godin, Benoît. 2006. "The linear model of innovation: The historical construction of an analytical framework." *Science, Technology, and Human Values* 31 (6): 639–67.

Godin, Benoît. 2017. *Models of Innovation: The History of an Idea.* Cambridge, MA: MIT Press.

Greater Kansas City Chamber. 2011. "Greater KC Chamber rolls out 'Big 5': Champions step up to lead Big 5 Initiatives." Accessed June 15, 2011 at http://www.big5kc.com/wp-content/uploads/2012/01/Big-5-5.pdf.

Greenstein, Shane. 2015. *How the Internet Became Commercial.* Princeton, NJ: Princeton University Press.

Griliches, Zvi. 1990. "Patent statistics as economic indicators: A survey." *Journal of Economic Literature* 28 (4): 1661–1707.

Griliches, Zvi. 1992. "The search for R&D spillovers." *Scandinavian Journal of Economics* 94 (supplement): 29–47.

Griliches, Zvi, Bronwyn H. Hall, and Ariel Pakes. 1991. "R&D, patents, and market value revisited: Is there a second (technological opportunity) factor?" *Economics of Innovation and New Technology* 1 (3): 183–201.

Grilli, Luca and Samuele Murtinu. 2014. "Government, venture capital, and the growth of European high-tech entrepreneurial firms." *Research Policy* 43 (9): 1523–43.

Grupp, Hariolf and Mary Ellen Mogee. 2004. "Indicators for national science and technology policy: How robust are composite indicators?" *Research Policy* 33: 1373–84.

Haltiwanger, John. 2012. "Job creation and firm dynamics in the U.S." *Innovation Policy and the Economy* 12: 17–38.

Haltiwanger, John, Ron S. Jarmin, and Javier Miranda. 2013. "Who creates jobs? Small vs. large vs. young." *Review of Economics and Statistics* 95 (2): 347–61.

Hannon, Paul D. 2003. "A conceptual development framework for management and leadership learning in the UK Incubator sector." *Education and Training* 45 (8/9): 449–60.

Harrison, Richard T. and Claire Leitch. 2010. "Voodoo institution or entrepreneurial university? Spin-off companies, the entrepreneurial system and regional development in the UK." *Regional Studies* 44 (9): 1241–62.

Hathaway, Ian. 2013. *Tech Starts: High-Technology Business Formation and Job Creation in the United States* (Kauffman Foundation Research Series). Kansas City, MO: Kauffman Foundation.

Hathaway, Ian and Robert Litan. 2014. *Declining Business Dynamism in the United States: A Look at States and Metros* (Economic Studies at Brookings). Washington DC: Brookings Institute.

Hecker, Daniel E. 2005. "High-technology employment: A NAICS-based update." *Monthly Labor Review* (July): 57–72.

HEMP. 2011. *Entrepreneurs + Mentors = Success: 22 Convincing Stories*. Kansas City, MO: Rockhill Books.

Henderson, J. Vernon. 1986. "Efficiency of resource usage and city size." *Journal of Urban Economics* 19 (1): 47–70.

Henderson, J. Vernon. 2003. "Marshall's scale economies." *Journal of Urban Economics* 53 (1): 1–28.

Hino, Satoshi. 2002. *A Study of Toyota Management System: Principles for Continuous Growth* [Toyota Keiei Sisutemu No Kenkyu: Eizokuteki Seicho No Genri]. Tokyo: Diamond Inc.

Hounshell, David. 2004. "Industrial research, commentary." In Karl Grandin and Nina Wormbs (eds.), *Reflections on the History and Historiography of Science and Research in Industry in the 20th Century*. Sagamore Beach, MA: Science History Publications, pp. 59–65.

Huffington Post. 2011. "The 8 best entrepreneurs to follow on Twitter." Accessed August 2, 2011 at http://www.huffingtonpost.com/scott-gerber/the-8-best-entrepreneurs-_b_912809.html.

Isard, Walter. 1956. *Location and Space-Economy*. Cambridge, MA: MIT Press.

Isenberg, Daniel. 2011. "Introducing the entrepreneurship ecosystem: Four defining characteristics." Forbes Leadership. Accessed February 4, 2019 at http://www.forbes.com/sites/danisenberg/2011/05/25/introducing-the-entrepreneurship-ecosystem-four-defining-characteristics/#4d6d2b4338c4.

Jaffe, Adam B., Michael S. Fogarty, and Bruce A. Banks. 1998. "Evidence from patents and patent citations on the impact of NASA and other federal labs on commercial innovation." *Journal of Industrial Economics* XLVI: 183–205.

Jaffe, Adam B. and Manuel Trajtenberg. 1996. Flows of knowledge from universities and federal labs: Modeling the flows of patent citations over time and across institutional and geographic boundaries. NBER Working Paper. Cambridge, MA: NBER.

Jaffe, Adam B. and Manuel Trajtenberg. 2002. *Patents, Citations, and Innovations: A Window on the Knowledge Economy*. Cambridge, MA: MIT Press.

Jaffe, Adam B., Manuel Trajtenberg, and Rebecca Henderson. 1993. "Geographic location of knowledge spillovers as evidenced by patent citations." *Quarterly Journal of Economics* 63 (3): 577–98.

Kansas City Area Life Sciences Institute. 2016. *Industry Census 2015.* Kansas City, MO.

Kask, Christopher and Edward Sieber. 2002. "Productivity growth in 'high-tech' manufacturing industries." *Monthly Labor Review* (March): 16–31.

KC Animal Health Corridor. 2016. "About the corridor." Accessed October 6, 2016 at http://kcanimalhealth.thinkkc.com/about.

KCSourceLink. 2017. "About KCSourceLink." Accessed January 26, 2017 at http://www.kcsourcelink.com/about-us/about-kcsourcelink.

Keeble, David and Sheila Walker. 1994. "New firms, small firms and dead firms: Spatial patterns and determinants in the United Kingdom." *Regional Studies* 28 (4): 411–27.

Kenney, Martin. 2000. *Understanding Silicon Valley: The Anatomy of an Entrepreneurial Region.* Palo Alto, CA: Stanford University Press.

King, Adam. 2002. "Mississippian period: Overview." Accessed December 20, 2018 at http://www.georgiaencyclopedia.org/artic les/history-archaeology/mississippian-period-overview.

Kleinknecht, Alfrad and Pierre Mohnen. 2002. *Innovation and Firm Performance: Econometric Explorations of Survey Data.* New York: Palgrave.

Kline, Stephen J. 1985. "Innovation is not a linear process." *Research Management* 28 (4): 36–45.

Kline, Stephen J. and Nathan Rosenberg. 2009. "An overview of innovation." In Nathan Rosenberg (ed.), *Studies on Science and the Innovation Process.* Oakland, CA: World Scientific, pp. 173–203.

Knowlton, Brian. 1996. "Boeing to buy McDonnell Douglas." *New York Times*, December 16. Accessed February 4, 2019 at www.nytimes.com/1996/12/16/news/16iht-merge.t_0.html.

Konczal, Jared and Yasuyuki Motoyama. 2013. "Energizing an ecosystem: Brewing 1 million cups." Kauffman Foundation Research Series. Kansas City, MO: Kauffman Foundation.

Kondratiev, Nikolai D. 1924. "Long waves in economic life." *Reviews of Economic Statistics* 17: 105–15.

Kossinets, Gueorgi. 2006. "Effects of missing data in social networks." *Social Networks* 28 (3): 247–68.

Lecuyer, Christophe. 2006. *Making Silicon Valley: Innovation and the Growth of High Tech, 1930–1970*. Cambridge, MA: MIT Press.

Lee, Sam Youl, Richard Florida, and Zoltan Acs. 2004. "Creativity and entrepreneurship: A regional analysis of new firm formation." *Regional Studies* 38 (8): 879–91.

Lerner, Joshua. 2002. "When bureaucrats meet entrepreneurs: The design of effective 'public venture capital' programmes." *Economic Journal* 112 (477): F73–84.

Lerner, Joshua. 2009. *Boulevard of Broken Dreams: Why Public Efforts to Boost Entrepreneurship and Venture Capital Have Failed and What to Do about It*. Princeton, NJ: Princeton University Press.

LeRoy, Greg. 2005. *Great American Job Scams: Corporate Tax Dodging and the Myth of Job Creation*. San Francisco, CA: Berrett-Koehler Publishers.

Lester, Richard. 2005. *Universities, Innovation, and the Competitiveness of Local Economies* (IPC Working Paper Series). Cambridge, MA: Industrial Performance Center, MIT.

Lester, Richard K. 2008. "Comment on 'commercialising university research: The Oxford model.'" *Capitalism and Society* 3 (1): 1–5.

Lettl, Christopher, Corneilius Herstatt, and Hans Georg Gemuenden. 2006. "Users' contributions to radical innovation: Evidence from four cases in the field of medical equipment technology." *R&D Management* 36 (3): 251–72.

Levy, Steven. 2011. *In the Plex*. New York: Simon and Schuster.

Li, Minghao, Stephan J. Goetz, Mark D. Partridge, and David A. Fleming. 2016. "Location determinants of high-growth firms." *Entrepreneurship and Regional Development* 28 (1–2): 97–125.

Liker, Jeffrey K. 2004. *Toyota Way: 14 Management Principles from the World's Greatest Manufacturer*. New York: McGraw-Hill.

Liu, Xielin and Stephen White. 2001. "Comparing innovation systems: A framework and application to China's transitional context." *Research Policy* 30 (7): 1091–1114.

Low, Sarah A. and Andrew M. Isserman. 2015. "Where are the innovative entrepreneurs? Identifying innovative industries and measuring innovative entrepreneurship." *International Regional Science Review* 38 (2): 171–201.

Lundvall, Bengt-Ake. 1992. *National Systems of Innovation: Towards a Theory of Innovation and Interactive Learning*. London: St. Martin's Press.

Lundvall, Bengt-Ake. 2010. *National Systems of Innovation: Toward a Theory of Innovation and Interactive Learning*. London: Anthem Press.

Lundvall, Bengt-Ake and Peter Maskell. 2000. "Nation states and economic development: From national systems of production to national systems of knowledge creation and learning." In Gordon L. Clark, Maryann P. Feldman, and Meric S. Gertler (eds.), *Oxford Handbook of Economic Geography*. Oxford: Oxford University Press, pp. 353–72.

Lyles, Ward. 2015. "Using social network analysis to examine planner involvement in environmentally oriented planning processes led by non-planning professions." *Journal of Environmental Planning and Management* 58 (11): 1961–87.

McCray, W. Patrick. 2005. "Will small be beautiful? Making policies for our nanotech future." *History and Technology* 21 (2): 177–203.

McNeil, Ronald D., Jung Jowe, Ted Mastroianni, Joseph Cronin, and Dyanne Ferk. 2007. "Barriers to nanotechnology commercialization: Final report." Prepared for US Department of Commerce, Technology Administration. Springfield, IL: University of Illinois at Springfield.

Mahr, Dominik and Annouk Lievens. 2012. "Virtual lead user communities: Drivers of knowledge creation for innovation." *Research Policy* 41 (1): 167–77.

Malecki, Edward J. 1993. "Entrepreneurship in regional and local development." *International Regional Science Review* 16 (1–2): 119–53.

Malecki, Edward J. 2009. "Geographical environments for entrepreneurship." *International Journal of Entrepreneurship and Small Business* 7 (2): 175–90.

Malizia, Emil and Yasuyuki Motoyama. 2016. "The economic development – vibrant center connection: Tracking high-growth firms in the D.C. region." *Professional Geographer* 68 (3): 349–55.

Malizia, Emil and Yasuyuki Motoyama. 2019. "Vibrant centers as locations for high-growth firms: An analysis of 30 U.S. metropolitan areas." *Professional Geographer* 71 (1): 15–28.

Markusen, Ann R., Yong-Sook Lee, and Sean DiGiovanna. 1999. *Second Tier Cities: Rapid Growth Beyond the Metropolis, Globalization and Community*, vol. 3. Minneapolis, MN: University of Minnesota Press.

Marshall, Alfred. 1898. *Principles of Economics*, 4th edn. 6 vols. London: Macmillan and Company.

Martin, Ron and Peter Sunley. 2003. "Deconstructing clusters: Chaotic concept or policy panacea?" *Journal of Economic Geography* 3: 5–35.

Mashable. 2009. "10 essential entrepreneurs to follow on Twitter." Accessed July 12, 2018 at http://mashable.com/2009/10/29/entre preneurs-twitter-follow/.

Mason, Colin. 2015. "Promoting entrepreneurship in peripheral regions: The limits to public sector venture capital funds." Paper to the First Learned Society for Wales International Symposium. Portmeirion, Wales.

Mayer, Heike. 2011. *Entrepreneurship and Innovation in Second Tier Regions*. Cheltenham: Edward Elgar Publishing.

Mayer, Heike. 2013. *The Evolution of Entrepreneurship in Kansas City: A Visual Approach to Analyzing Entrepreneurial Development* (Kauffman Foundation Paper Series). Kansas City, MO: Ewing Marion Kauffman Foundation.

Mody, Cyrus. 2006. "Corporations, universities, and instrumental communities: Commercializing probe microscopy, 1981–1996." *Technology and Culture* 47 (1): 56–80.

Motoyama, Yasuyuki. 2008. "What was new about the cluster theory?: What could it answer and what could it not answer?" *Economic Development Quarterly* 22: 353–63.

Motoyama, Yasuyuki. 2012. *Global Companies, Local Innovations: Why the Engineering Aspects of Innovation Making Requires Proximity* (Economic Geography Series). Farnham: Ashgate.

Motoyama, Yasuyuki. 2015. "The state-level analysis of high-growth firms." *Journal of Small Business and Entrepreneurship* 27 (2): 213–27.

Motoyama, Yasuyuki, Richard P. Appelbaum, and Rachel Parker. 2011. "The National Nanotechnology Initiative: Federal Support for Science and Technology, or Hidden Industrial Policy?" *Technology in Society* 33 (1–2): 109–18.

Motoyama, Yasuyuki, Cong Cao, and Richard P. Appelbaum. 2014. "Observing regional divergence of Chinese nanotechnology centers." *Technological Forecasting and Social Change* 81 (1): 11–21.

Motoyama, Yasuyuki, Brian Danley, Jordan Bell-Masterson, Kate Maxwell, and Arnobio Morelix. 2013. *Leveraging Regional Assets: Insights from High-Growth Companies in Kansas City* (Kauffman Foundation Research Paper). Kansas City, MO: Kauffman Foundation.

Motoyama, Yasuyuki, Stephan Goetz, and Yicheol Han. 2018. "Where do entrepreneurs get information? An analysis of Twitter-following patterns." *Journal of Small Business and Entrepreneurship* 30 (3): 253–74.

Motoyama, Yasuyuki and Karren Knowlton. 2016. "From resource munificence to ecosystem integration: The case of government sponsorship in St. Louis." *Entrepreneurship and Regional Development* 28 (5–6): 448–70.

Motoyama, Yasuyuki and Emil Malizia. 2017. "Demand pull or supply push? Metro-level analysis of start-ups in the U.S." *Regional Studies, Regional Science* 4 (1): 232–46.

Motoyama, Yasuyuki and Heike Mayer. 2017. "Revisiting the role of university in regional economic development: A triangulation of data." *Growth and Change* 48 (4): 787–804.

Mowery, David. 2009. "Nanotechnology: A new wave of the U.S. national innovation system?" Keynote speech at the Society for the Study of Nanoscience and Emerging Technologies (S.Net). December 9, Seattle, WA.

Mueller, Pamela. 2007. "Exploiting entrepreneurial opportunities: The impact of entrepreneurship on growth." *Small Business Economics* 28 (4): 355–62.

Mueller, Pamela, Andre Van Stel, and David J. Storey. 2008. "The effects of new firm formation on regional development over time: the case of Great Britain." *Small Business Economics* 30 (1): 59–71.

NBIA. 2011. "Annual report." Athens, OH: National Business Incubation Association.

Neck, Heidi M., G. Dale Meyer, Boyd Cohen, and Andrew Corbett. 2004. "An entrepreneurial system view of new venture creation." *Journal of Small Business Management* 42 (2): 190–208.

Nelson, Richard R. 1993. *National Innovation Systems: A Comparative Analysis.* New York: Oxford University Press.

NESTA. 2009. *The Vital 6 Percent: How High-Growth Innovative Business Generate Prosperity and Jobs.* London: NESTA.

NextWeb. 2011. "25 most influential people tweeting about entrepreneurship." Accessed April 11, 2011 at http://thenextweb.com/socialmedia/2011/04/21/the-25-most-influential-people-tweeting-about-entrepreneurship/.

Nibletz. 2011. "50 startup related twitter accounts to follow." Accessed July 12, 2011 at http://nibletz.com/2013/07/12/follow-friday-50-startup-related-twitter-accounts-follow/.

Nightingale, Paul. 1998. "A cognitive model of innovation." *Research Policy* 27 (7): 689–709.

Nightingale, Paul, Gordon Murray, Marc Cowling, Charles Baden-Fuller, Colin Mason, Josh Siepel, Mike Hopkins, and Charles Dannreuther. 2009. *From Funding Gaps to Thin Markets: UK Government Support for Early-Stage Venture Capital.* London: NESTA.

North, Douglass. 1987. "Institutions, transaction costs and economic growth." *Economic Inquiry* 25 (3): 419–28.

North, Douglass. 1990. *Institutions, Institutional Change and Economic Performance.* Cambridge: Cambridge University Press.

Norton, R.D. 1992. "Agglomeration and competitiveness: From Marshall to Chinitz." *Urban Studies* 29 (2): 155–70.

NSF (National Science Foundation). 1953. "Science and public policy." In *Annual Report of the National Science Foundation.* Washington DC: National Science Foundation.

NSF (National Science Foundation). 2012. "Science and engineering indicators." Washington DC: National Science Board.

NSF (National Science Foundation). 2018. "Science and engineering indicators." Washington DC: National Science Board.

NVCA. 2016. "Who we are." National Venture Capital Association. Accessed November 18, 2016 at http://nvca.org/about-nvca/who-we-are/.

Nylon Schooter. 2014. "Profile of Shooter, Michael Jordan." Accessed February 4, 2019 at http://nyloncalculus.com/2014/08/18/profile-shooter-michael-jordan/.

OECD. 1997. "Revision of the high-technology sector and product classification." Paper by Thomas Hatzichronoglou. Paris: Organisation for Economic Cooperation and Development.

OECD. 2002. *Frascati Manual: Proposed Standard Practice for Surveys on Research and Experimental Development.* Paris: Organisation for Economic Cooperation and Development.

OECD. 2010. *High-Growth Enterprises: What Governments Can Do to Make a Difference.* Paris: Organisation for Economic Cooperation and Development.

Ohio State University. 2018. "Technology commercialization office: What is our mission?" Presentation by Rick Smith, August 17. Columbus, OH.

Ó hUallacháin, Breandán. 1999. "Patent places: Size matters." *Journal of Regional Science* 39 (4): 613–36.

Parida, Vinit, Mats Westerberg, and Johan Frishammar. 2012. "Inbound open innovation activities in high-tech SMEs: The impact on innovation performance." *Journal of Small Business Management* 50 (2): 283–309.

Patton, Donald and Martin Kenney. 2010. "The role of the university in the genesis and evolution of research-based clusters." In Dirk Fornahl, Sebastian Henn, and Max-Peter Menzel (eds.), *Emerging Clusters: Theoretical, Empirical and Political Perspectives on the Initial Stage of Cluster Evolution*. Cheltenham: Edward Elgar Publishing, pp. 214–38.

Pederson, Jay P. 2000. *International Directory of Company Histories*. Detroit, MI: St. James Press.

Porter, Michael E. 1990. *The Competitive Advantage of Nations*. New York: Free Press.

Porter, Michael E. 1994. "The role of location in competition." *Journal of the Economics of Business* 1 (1): 35–9.

Porter, Michael E. 1998. "Clusters and the new economics of competition." *Harvard Business Review* 76 (6): 77–90.

Porter, Michael E. 2000. "Location, competition, and economic development: Local clusters in a global economy." *Economic Development Quarterly* 14 (1): 15–34.

PricewaterhouseCoopers, and National Venture Capital Association. 2011. MoneyTree Report. PricewaterhouseCoopers.

PricewaterhouseCoopers, and National Venture Capital Association. 2015. MoneyTree Report. PricewaterhouseCoopers.

Primm, James Neal. 1998. *Lion of the Valley: St. Louis, Missouri, 1764–1980*, 3rd edn. St. Louis, MO: Missouri History Museum.

Prügl, Reinhard and Martin Schreier. 2006. "Learning from leading-edge customers at the Sims: Opening up the innovation process using toolkits." *R&D Management* 36 (3): 237–50.

Qian, Haifeng and Xin Yao. 2017. "The role of research universities in U.S. college-town entrepreneurial ecosystems." SSRN Working Paper.

Quigley, John. 2002. "Introduction." Presentation in Housing and Urban Economics, August. Berkeley, CA.

Ratanawaraha, Apiwat and Karen R. Polenske. 2007. "Measuring the geography of innovation: A literature review." In Karen R. Polenske (ed.), *Economic Geography of Innovation*. Cambridge: Cambridge University Press, pp. 30–59.

Reynolds, Paul D. 1994. "Autonomous firm dynamics and economic growth in the United States, 1986–1990." *Regional Studies* 28 (4): 429–42.

Rice, Murray D., Sean O'Hagan, Chetan Tiwari, Donald Lyons, Milford B. Green, and Vicki Oppenheim. 2017. "Defining the record of high-growth firms by metropolitan region: What happens to the Inc. 500?" *Papers in Applied Geography* 4 (2): 137–56.

Rodrik, Dani. 2014. "Green industrial policy." *Oxford Review of Economic Policy* 30 (3): 469–91.

Saxenian, AnnaLee. 1994. *Regional Advantage: Culture and Competition in Silicon Valley and Route 128*. Cambridge, MA: Harvard University Press.

Saxenian, AnnaLee. 1999. *Silicon Valley's New Immigrant Entrepreneurs*. San Francisco, CA: Public Policy Institute of California.

SBA. 2011. Frequently Asked Questions. In *Advocacy: the voice of small business in government*. Washington DC: Small Business Administration, Office of Advocacy.

SBA. 2012. "Firm survival rates." Small Business Administration. Accessed January 10, 2019 at www.bls.gov/bdm/us_age_naics_00_table7.txt.

Schumpeter, Joseph Alois. 1934 [2012]. *The Theory of Economic Development: An Inquiry into Profits, Capital, Credit, Interest, and the Business Cycle*, 10th edn. New Brunswick, NJ: Transaction Books.

Schumpeter, Joseph Alois. 1939. *Business Cycles: A Theoretical, Historical, and Statistical Analysis of the Capitalist Process*, 1st edn. New York: McGraw-Hill Book Company.

Schumpeter, Joseph Alois. 1954. *History of Economic Analysis*. New York: Oxford University Press.

Shortridge, James R. 2012. *Kansas City and How it Grew, 1822–2011*. Lawrence, KS: University of Kansas Press.

Sledzik, Karol. 2013. Schumpeter's view on innovation and entrepreneurship. SSRN Working Paper.

Smith, Keith. 2005. "Measuring innovation." In Jan Fagerberg, David C. Mowery, and Richard R. Nelson (eds.), *The Oxford Handbook of Innovation*. Oxford: Oxford University Press, pp. 148–77.

Spigel, Ben. 2016. "Relational organization of entrepreneurial ecosystems." *Entrepreneurship Theory and Practice* 41 (1): 49–72.

Spigel, Ben. 2017. "Bourdieu, culture, and the economic geography of practice: Entrepreneurial mentorship in Ottawa and Waterloo, Canada." *Journal of Economic Geography* 17 (2): 287–310.

Spigel, Ben and Richard Harrison. 2018. "Toward a process theory of entrepreneurial ecosystems." *Strategic Management Journal* 12 (1): 151–68.

Stam, Erik. 2015. "Entrepreneurial ecosystems and regional policy: A sympathetic critique." *European Planning Studies* 23 (9): 1759–69.

Stam, Erik and Ben Spigel. 2018. "Entrepreneurial ecosystems." In R. Blackburn, D. De Clercq, J. Heinonen, and Z. Wang (eds.), *Sage Handbook for Entrepreneurship and Small Business*. Thousand Oaks, CA: Sage, chapter 21.

Stowers Institute. 2016. "Quick facts." Accessed October 6, 2018 at http://www.stowers.org/about/factsheet.

T-Rex. 2017. "About T-Rex." Accessed February 20, 2017 at http://www.downtowntrex.org/about/.

Tall.life. 2018. "Height percentile calculator, by age or country." Accessed February 4, 2019 at https://tall.life/height-percentile-calculator-age-country/.

Taylor, Frederick Winslow. 1903. *Shop Management: A Paper Read before the American Society of Mechanical Engineers*. New York and London: Harper & Brothers.

Taylor, Frederick Winslow. 1911. *The Principles of Scientific Management*. London: Harper & Brothers.

Top End Sports.com. 2018. "Vertical jump test results." Accessed February 4, 2019 at www.topendsports.com/testing/results/vertical-jump.htm.

Trillin, Calvin. 2011. *Quite Enough of Calvin Trillin*. New York: Random House.

Under30CEO. 2011. "25 Twitter chats every entrepreneur must know." Accessed October 26, 2011 at http://under30ceo.com/25-twitter-chats-every-entrepreneur-must-know/.

University of Maryland. 2010. "University technology transfer." College Park, MD: University of Maryland, Office of Technology Commercialization. Accessed September 18, 2018 at http://otc.umd.edu/sites/default/files/documents/about-otc-2010.pdf.

USPTO. 1985. "General Information Concerning Patents."

USPTO. 1995. "General Information Concerning Patents."

USPTO. 2005. "General Information Concerning Patents."

USPTO. 2014. "General Information Concerning Patents."

USPTO (US Patent and Trademark Office). 2015. "General information concerning patents." Accessed December 14, 2018 at www.

uspto.gov/patents-getting-started/general-information-concerning-patents.

USPTO (US Patent and Trademark Office). 2016. "U.S. patent statistics chart: Calendar years 1963–2015." Accessed May 3, 2018 at http://www.uspto.gov/web/offices/ac/ido/oeip/taf/us_stat. htm.

Van de Ven, Andrew. 1993. "The development of an infrastructure for entrepreneurship." *Journal of Business Venturing* 8: 211–30.

Van Stel, Andre and Kashifa Suddle. 2008. "The effects of new firm formation on regional development in the Netherlands." *Small Business Economics* 30 (1): 31–47.

Varga, Attila. 1999. "Time–space patterns of US innovation – Stability of change?" In Manfred M. Fischer, Luis Suarea-Villa, and Michael Steiner (eds.), *Innovation, Networks and Localities*. New York: Springer, pp. 215–34.

Von Hippel, Eric. 1976. "The dominant role of users in the scientific instrument innovation process." *Research Policy* 5 (3): 212–39.

Von Hippel, Eric and Ralph Katz. 2002. "Shifting innovation to users via toolkits." *Management Science* 48 (7): 821–33.

Weber, Steve. 2004. *The Success of Open Source*. Cambridge, MA: Harvard University Press.

Wyandotte County. 2016. "History of Lewis & Clark at Kaw Point." Wyandotte County Lewis & Clark Task Force. Accessed December 20, 2016 at http://www.lewisandclarkwyco.org/lewis-clark/camp-at-kaw-point.

Zook, Matthew. 2005. *The Geography of the Internet Industry*. Oxford: Wiley.

Zucker, Lynne G. and Michael R. Darby. 1996. "Star scientists and institutional transformation: Patterns of invention and innovation in the formation of the biotech industry." *Proceedings of the National Academy of Science* 93: 12709–16.

Zucker, Lynne G., Michael R. Darby, and Marilyn B. Brewer. 1998. "Intellectual human capital and the birth of U.S. biotechnology enterprises." *American Economic Review* 88 (1): 290–306.

Zucker, Lynne G., Michael R. Darby, Jonathan Furner, Robert C. Liu, and Hongyan Ma. 2007. "Minerva unbound: Knowledge stocks, knowledge flows and new knowledge production." *Research Policy* 36: 850–63.

Index

Acs, Z. 12, 17–19, 22–3, 28–9, 34,
    39
Amezcua, A.S. 129, 131, 136
anchor companies 6, 43, 60–61, 78,
    83
Application Developers Alliance 99
Arch Grants
    aim to promote and celebrate
        entrepreneurship 61, 131,
        136
    background to 63–4
    business plan competition 114
    connectivity at multiple levels
        134
    as "great environment" for
        startups 122
    interactions
        beyond industrial sector 66
        proximity to enhance 66–7, 90
    knowledge exchange 115–16
    as major support organization 62
    number of participants
        interviewed 132
    peer-based learning 64–5, 90,
        116–17
    performance of firms 114–15
    recipients and supports
        location of 68
        network map of 70
    scaling up companies 120
    seed money 120, 131
    support
        collaboration and
            co-ordination between
            organizations of 71–2,
            124
        multiple layers of 67–71, 123
        psychological 65–6
    Twitter accounts 99, 111, 123

Association for University
    Technology Managers
    (AUTM) 127, 138–9
Audretsch, D.B. 12–13, 17, 19, 23,
    31, 34, 39

"big business" city 60
BioGenerator 62, 71
BioSTL 61–2, 69–70, 106, 109
bootstrapping 3, 87–91, 120, 129,
    131
Business Dynamics Statistics
    (BDS)
    limitations of data 29
    longevity of new firms 134
    metropolitan areas 35
    in regression analysis 35, 144
    reliability of data 29
    revealing sharp rise of startup
        activities in St. Louis 61
    startup rates in all industries 30,
        144
business mentors 81–4, 91, 111–12,
    117
business plan competition 6, 63–5,
    114, 130, 139
business plans 115, 130–31, 138
business service companies 77–85,
    114, 117–18

Cambridge Innovation Center
    (CIC) 1, 62, 121, 136
Capital Innovators 61–2, 67–8,
    71–2, 99, 106, 111, 123–4
Center for Emerging Technologies
    62, 69, 99, 106, 111, 123
City of Fountains *see* Kansas City
co-ordination
    between ESOs 124–5

between support organizations
71–2, 90
collaboration
at local level 55–6
between support organizations
71–2
vertical 13
communities of Twitter accounts
Kansas City 103–7, 110–11, 123
St. Louis 106–12, 123
connectivity
Arch Grants as locus of 64
embed in entrepreneurial context
recommendation 134–5
universities' ability to 139
between entrepreneurs and
support organizations as
crucial 137
facilitating local 55–6
increase within regions
recommendation 134
universities' ability to 139
organized at regional level 42
as primary source of
entrepreneurship
development 140
as process activity 140
social media and content analysis
enriching 141
continuous learning 4–5
CORTEX 61–2, 67, 90
Cultivation Capital 61–2, 71–2, 109,
111, 123

data for entrepreneurship 139–41
Defense Advanced Research
Projects Agency (DARPA)
128
Drucker, P.F. 9–10, 19

Economic Development
Administration (EDA) 127–8
ecosystem catalysis 56–7, 58
ecosystem studies 24–5
Edquist, C. 8–9, 11–12
entrepreneurs
captivating 136–7

classic versus casual styles 1–4,
113
cultivating variety of sources
123–4, 129, 132
defining 9–10
developing and using new
technologies 13, 131
ESOs
benefitting from co-ordination
between 124–5
importance of 121–2
go-to place for 56, 58, 95, 135
importance of learning 4–5,
115–16, 136
importance of peer- and mentor-
based feedback and support
organizations 116–18
interviews
1 Million Cups 52–8, 116, 132
Arch Grants 63–92, 132, 134
local learning system 122–3
multiple layers of support for
lone 67–71
as people who create inventions
20
as people who execute business
plans 130
as people who start new
companies 20–21
power of incremental and
internal growth 120–21,
131
role to identify market niche
118–20, 130
Twitter accounts 94–7, 103–8,
111–12
universities increasing
connectivity of 139
entrepreneurship
5-50 rule 3–4, 114
as buzzword 9–10
caveats and analogy 132–4
commercialization opportunities
13
concept 8–10
data for 139–41
definition 9

differentiating with innovation
9–10, 20, 22, 125
as driven by human-based
activities 41–2
as driver of economic
development 21–2
ecosystem studies 24–5
future research avenues 141
iceberg analogy 133–4
just-in-time production system
and 137–8
as largely local phenomenon 22
local system of 25–6, 110, 123–4,
141
measures of
areas covered 35
correlation with purchasing
power 34
establishment-based 28–9
Inc. firms 31, 33
new firm creation in all
industries 29–30
new firm creation in high-tech
industries 29, 31–2
regression analysis 35–41,
142–4
research activities 34
self-employment 27–8
as output and process 20–26
policy recommendations
avoiding provision of full
services 136–7
avoiding public venture funds
and incubators 136
creating go-to place for
entrepreneurs 135
embedding connectivity 134–5
increasing connectivity within
regions 134
regional factors associated with
22–3, 41, 48
as risky business with major
reorientation 114–15
role of universities 139
Twitter accounts related to
information sources followed
95–103

Kansas City 103–7, 110–11,
123
possibility of hidden 112
St. Louis 106–12, 123
entrepreneurship model
comparison with innovation
model 129–32
summary of 129
entrepreneurship support
organizations (ESOs)
co-ordination between 124–5
importance of 121–2
Kansas City 104–7, 110, 123
network connections 70
St. Louis 62, 106, 109, 111, 123
Twitter accounts 96–8, 100,
104–7, 109–11, 123
see also support organizations
establishment-based measure
28–9

5-50 rule 3–4, 114
Feldman, M.P. 12–13, 16–17,
19–20, 22, 24, 31
Freeman, C. 9, 11, 16

Gateway City *see* St. Louis
"go-getters" 84, 91
go-to place for entrepreneurs 56,
58, 95, 135
Godin, B. 7, 14, 126, 140
government
role of 7, 128
Twitter accounts 96–7, 100–107,
109–11
government support
Inc. firms 89
ineffectiveness 128–9
linear model in 127–8
provision of seed money 129
research funding 34, 38, 40, 66,
133, 139
growth
based on market niche 75–8,
90–91, 119
incremental 87, 91, 120–21, 129,
131

in innovation and
   entrepreneurship models
   129, 131
waves of 10

health companies 76–8, 81, 84–6,
   119, 132
Helzberg Entrepreneurship
   Mentorship Program (HEMP)
   82–3, 117
"hidden industrial policy" 128
high-growth companies
   definition 31
   facing pivots 114
   hyper growth and survival 133–4
   interviews in Kansas City and St.
      Louis 72–92, 145
   model
      college completion rate 39
      map of firm ratios 33
      regression analysis 35–7, 142–4
      significance of SBIR 38
      similarity to high-tech startup
         model 37
      VC-type investment 38–9, 120
   prior studies on 25
   valuing business mentors 117
high-tech
   as not driving economy through
      entrepreneurship 40
   synonymy with innovation 19–20
high-tech companies
   bias towards as cause of
      ineffectiveness 128–9
   Kansas City
      as home to 43–4
      survey of 45–51, 57–8, 119
high-tech industries
   as innovation measure 15–16, 18
   new firm creation, as measure of
      entrepreneurship 29, 31–2
high-tech model
   college completion rate 39
   population flux 39–40
   regression analysis 35–7, 142–4
   similarity to high-growth firm
      model 37

universities 38
use of variables 34
VC-type investment 38
human capital
   education level and population
      flux as factors of 40
   as element of local
      entrepreneurship ecosystem
      24
   importance of 39
   innovation as function of 34
   startup activities and 35
human transfer 138–9

iceberg analogy 133–4
Inc. firms
   as entrepreneurship measure 31,
      33
   financial sources 89
   as high-growth firms 31
   interviews
      advantages 73
      bootstrapping and self-finance
         87–91, 120
      business mentors 81–4, 91, 117
      changes and pivots 78–81, 91,
         114–15
      cities conducted in 73–5, 122–3
      descriptive statistics 74
      growth based on market niche
         75–8, 90–91, 119
      locally recruited and trained
         talent 84–7, 91–2
      number of participants 132
      target firms 73
   map of firm ratios 33
   regression analysis 35–7, 142–4
   results 38–42
incremental growth 87, 91, 120–21,
   129, 131
incubators
   aim to provide comprehensive
      service 131–2
   recommendation to re-tailor
      operations 136
   role of public sector 131
   in St. Louis 62

survival during incubated period
129
T-Rex functioning as 61, 66–7,
121
individual company level
entrepreneurs having to learn
115–16
entrepreneurship as risky 114–15
identifying market niche 118–20
importance of peer- and mentor-
based feedback and support
organizations 116–18
power of incremental and
internal growth 120–21
Innovate VMS 61, 71
innovation
as buzzword 9–10
as coming from something other
than research 47
definition 8–9, 74
differentiating with
entrepreneurship 9–10, 20,
22, 125
dominant approach to promoting
7
Kansas City having right assets
for 41, 44
measures and limitations 14–20,
140
in relation to knowledge spillover
12–14, 38
synonymy with high-tech 19–20
systems of innovation theory
10–12
see also linear model of
innovation
"innovative entrepreneurship"
sectors 28
interaction
beyond industrial sector 66
with business mentors 81–2
connectivity and 134–5
importance of embedding 136
local nature of 122–3
peer-based learning 53–4, 64–5,
115, 117
proximity to enhance 66–7, 90

psychological support 65–6
with specific universities 48–50,
57
internal growth 120–21
interviews
of 1 Million Cups entrepreneurs
52–8
advantages and drawbacks 141
of high-growth firms 72–92, 145
possibly having selection bias
119, 132
invention 8–9, 16, 119–20, 125–7
IT companies 75–6, 78, 80, 83–8,
117–18, 120–21
ITEN 61–2, 67–8, 71, 93, 109, 111,
121, 123, 135

Jaffe, A.B. 12, 16, 31
job creation 21–2, 27, 60–61, 89
just-in-time production system
137–8

Kansas City
background to 43–5, 59
having right assets for innovation
and entrepreneurship
activities 41
interviews of high-growth firms
72–92, 118, 120–22, 125,
135
as metropolitan area 43
multiple circles of mentorships
117
startup rates in 41–2
survey of high-tech firms 45–51,
57–8, 119
Twitter accounts
communities 103–7, 110–11,
123
most followed academic
accounts 102
most followed association
accounts 99
most followed ESO accounts
97–9
most followed government
accounts 100–102

most followed service
providers 100
number of entries 94
number of followers 95
number of sources 94–5
types of 96–7, 123
see also 1 Million Cups (1MC)
Kauffman, E.M. 6, 82–3, 117, 123,
136
Kauffman Foundation 6, 45, 52–3,
82, 94–5, 97, 99, 106, 110–11
KCSourceLink 94, 123
knowledge
"new" 14, 125
sharing 65
stock of 25–6
types to acquire 115–16
knowledge spillover
dependent variable 34
literature on 12–13, 20, 31, 34
taking place between
entrepreneurs 4
knowledge spillover theory 14, 23,
25, 38–9, 48
KU Med 48–9
see also University of Kansas
(KU)

Lab 1500 62, 69, 98–9, 109, 111
learning
continuous 4–5
experimental 116
importance for entrepreneurs
4–5, 115–16, 136
interviews for portraying nature
and level of 141
local system of 122–3
as process activity 116, 140
see also peer-based learning
linear model of innovation
assumed processes of 7, 125–6
caveats and analogy 132–4
comparison with
entrepreneurship model
129–32
current policy following 125, 129
in government support 127–8

ineffectiveness in 128–9
revisited and applied to
entrepreneurship 139–41
summary of 129
in technology commercialization
offices by universities 126–7
local connections, facilitation of
55–6
local learning system 122–3
locally recruited and trained talent
84–7

market niche
growth based on 75–8, 90–91, 119
identifying 118–20, 130
Marshall, A. 22
Mayer, H. 41, 43, 46, 50–51
measures
of entrepreneurship 27–35
of innovation 14–20
mentor-based feedback 116–18
mentors
contrasted to Twitter-based
relationship 111–12
presence of 81–4
as source of new ideas 48–50, 56
St. Louis 62, 68–9, 71
metropolitan areas
divided between two states 44
Kansas City as 30th largest US 43
number and definition of 35
regression results at level of 44–5,
92, 120
right assets for innovation
activities 41
startup rates 42
universities 38, 92
used as unit of analysis 29
Michael Jordan analogy 133
MIT 79, 119–20
Mosaic Project 61

National Establishment Time-
Series (NETS)
provision of detailed industry
information 29
in regression analysis 35–6, 144

startup rates in high-tech sectors 32, 144
National Institute of Standards and Technology (NIST) 25, 128
National Institutes of Health (NIH) 34, 38, 40, 70, 144
National Nanotechnology Initiative 128, 140
National Science Foundation (NSF) 14, 140
National Venture Capital Association (NVCA) 88–9
network analysis
  for community detection 103–8
  general Twitter following patterns 96–103
  methodology 93–5
  missing data due to non-response as problematic 95
  summary of results 108–11
new firm creation
  in all industries 29–30
  establishment-based data limitation 28
  in high-tech industries 29, 31–2
niche market *see* market niche

1 Million Cups (1MC)
  background to 52–3
  demographic attracted to 141
  difficulties of developing networks prior to attending 57–8, 122
  entrepreneur interviews
    ecosystem catalysis 56–7
    facilitating local connections 55–6, 58
    value of peer-to-peer learning 53–4, 57, 90, 116
  example of embedding connectivity 134–5
  as major support organization 62, 70
  number of participants interviewed 132
  serving as go-to place for entrepreneurs 56, 58, 95, 135

open innovation systems 13
output
  blurring with innovation input 19–20
  entrepreneurship as 20–26
  patents as measure of innovation 12, 17–18, 140
  of scientific and technological activities 14

patents
  entrepreneurship and 140
  as innovation measure 16–19
  innovation model 130, 132–3
  knowledge spillover and 12
  startup activities 35–9, 40, 42, 44–5, 144
  technology transfer office 126–7
  top US patent granted organizations 19
peer-based feedback 116–18
peer-based learning
  importance of
    1MC 53–4, 57, 90, 116
    Arch Grants 64–5, 90, 116–17
    interaction 53–4, 64–5, 115, 117
    psychological support 65–6
    value of 53–4, 57, 90, 116
peer-to-peer learning *see* peer-based learning
pivots and changes 78–81, 91, 114–15, 123, 131
policy and practice, current
  comparison of models 129–34
  linear model
    assumed processes of 7, 125–6
    in government support 127–8
    ineffectiveness in 128–9
    in technology commercialization offices by universities 126–7
  summary of models 129
policy implications
  data for entrepreneurship 139–41
  entrepreneurship and just-in-time production system 137–8
  future research avenues 141

from technology transfer to
human transfer 138–9
policy recommendations
avoid captivating entrepreneurs
or providing full services
136–7
avoid public venture funds and
incubators 136
connectivity
embed in entrepreneurial
context 134–5
increase within regions 134
create go-to place for
entrepreneurs 135
Porter, M.E. 11, 15–16, 22, 24, 110,
116
process
entrepreneurship as 20–26
learning as 116, 140
Prosper 61–2
proximity 66–7, 90
psychological support 65–6
public venture funds 136

R&D
entrepreneurship rates and 23
in high-tech sectors 45, 48–9
as innovation measure
activities 14–15, 19–20
intensity 15–16, 18–19
personnel and expenditure 14,
18
in life cycle of technology transfer
127
regional case studies *see* Kansas
City; St. Louis
regional clusters 40
regional divergence example 39
regional factors
associated with entrepreneurship
23, 41
for firms' development 47–8, 51,
57
regional industrial structure
22–3
Regional Innovation Strategies
(RIS) program 128

regional level
connectivity of entrepreneurs
organized at 42
cultivation of variety of sources
123–4
entrepreneurship support
organizations
co-ordination between 124–5
importance of 121–2
importance of role model
entrepreneurs 25
local learning system 122–3
recommendation to increase
connectivity 134
regional innovation system
11–12
stock of knowledge 25–6
Twitter accounts 97, 99, 110
where production and innovation
system is organized 11
regression analysis 35–37, 142–4
results 38–42

San Jose 41–2, 142
Sandia National Laboratories 128
Schumpeter, J.A. 8–10, 20–21, 74
seed money 128–9, 131–2
self-employment 27–8, 31
self-finance 87–90, 120
Silicon Valley 22, 29, 41, 60, 75
SixThirty 61–2
Skandalaris Center 62, 71–2, 93,
102–3, 106, 108–9, 111, 121,
124
Small Business Administration
(SBA) 13, 17–18, 100–101, 103,
105, 114, 128, 135
Small Business Innovation
Research (SBIR) 1–2, 35–8, 40,
66, 115–16, 144
St. Louis
Arch Grants
interaction beyond industrial
sector 66
multiple layers of support
67–71
peer-based learning 64–5

proximity to enhance
        interactions 66–7
    psychological support 65–6
    seed money 131
    and startup ecosystem 63–4
    background to 6, 59–61
    having right assets for innovation
        and entrepreneurship
        activities 41
    interviews of high-growth firms
        72–92, 117, 120–22
    level of entrepreneurship 6, 29
    major support organizations in
        co-ordination between 71–2,
        124–5
        location 68
        names 62
        network 70
        overlapping functions 124
    Twitter accounts
        communities 106–12, 123
        most followed academic
            accounts 102–3
        most followed association
            accounts 99
        most followed ESO accounts
            97–9
        most followed government
            accounts 100–102
        most followed service
            providers 100
        number of entries 94
        number of followers 95
        number of sources 94–5
        types of 96–7, 123
St. Louis Regional Chamber 61, 99,
    106, 109
startup companies
    in all industries 30, 35, 39, 144
    effects of little population growth
        of low flow of people 40
    in high-tech sectors 32, 35–6, 39,
        40, 144
    as net job creators in US 21
    rates in metro areas and US 41–2
    in St. Louis 63–72, 122
    university-based 129, 138–9

startup ecosystem 63–72
startup-related Twitter accounts
    94–9, 103, 105, 110–11
STL VentureWorks 71
support organizations
    collaboration and co-ordination
        between 71–2
    importance of 116–18
    see also entrepreneurship support
        organizations (ESOs)
surveys
    advantages and drawbacks 141
    of financial sources of *Inc.* firms
        89, 120
    of high-tech companies 45–51,
        57–8, 93, 132–3
    as innovation measure 17–18
    possibly having selection bias
        119, 132
systems of innovation theory 10–12,
    14

T-Rex 3, 61–2, 66–7, 90, 111, 121,
    136
talent
    locally recruited and trained
        84–7, 91–2
    technology 47–8, 50
Taylor, F.W. 137–8
technological infrastructure 20
technology commercialization
        offices
    bridging efforts 139–40
    ineffectiveness 128–9
    linear model in 126–7
    Twitter accounts 102
technology talent 47–8, 50
technology transfer 138–9
    see also technology
        commercialization offices
Twitter
    analysis
        advantages and drawbacks 141
        caution 110
        methodology of 93–5
        as novel 110
    community detection

Kansas City 103–6, 110–11,
        123
    St Louis 106–12, 123
    following patterns 96–103
    local nature of interaction
        reflected by 123
    summary of results 108–12

universities
    different roles in
        entrepreneurship 139
    generation of startups 129, 138–9
    interaction with 48–50, 57
    linear model in technology
        commercialization offices
        126–8
    local 79, 85, 91–2
    patents or licenses from regional
        132
    research 24–5, 34, 35–8, 40, 44,
        46, 51, 92, 139
    Twitter accounts 96, 102–3, 108,
        110
University of Kansas (KU) 44,
    48–50, 85, 92, 102, 107, 110
University of Missouri – Kansas
    City (UMKC) 44, 48–50, 85,
    102

US Patent and Trademark Office
    (USPTO) 1, 16, 19

"valley of death" 7, 128, 139
venture capital (VC)
    essential for entrepreneurial
        culture 24
    government role to provide
        128
    not prerequisite for firm growth
        25
    as significant research factor 35–6
    in St. Louis 62
venture capitalists (VCs)
    business plans and 130
    as financial source of *Inc.* firms
        89
    interviewed firms using finance
        from 88, 90
    known to invest in high-tech
        sectors and high-growth
        companies 38
    role of 88–9, 91, 120–21

Washington University (WashU)
    61–2, 72, 85, 92–3, 102–3, 106,
    108–9, 111, 121, 124
work ethic 86–7